THE 'VERY PURE WORD OF GOD'

THE BOOK OF COMMON PRAYER AS A MODEL OF BIBLICAL LITURGY

BY PETER ADAM

The Latimer Trust

The 'Very Pure Word of God': The Book of Common Prayer as a Model of Biblical Liturgy © Peter Adam 2012

ISBN 978-1-906327-09-5

Cover photo Canterbury Cathedral © Mark Physsas - Fotolia.com

Quotations from the Bible are taken from the *New Revised Standard Version Bible*, copyright 1989, Division of Christian Education of the National Council of the Churches of Christ in the United States of America.

Published by the Latimer Trust June 2012

The Latimer Trust
c/o Oak Hill College
London N14 4PS UK
Registered Charity: 1084337
Company Number: 4104465
Web: www.latimertrust.org
E-mail: administrator@latimertrust.org

Foreword to the Anglican Foundations Series

The celebration of the 350th anniversary of the 1662 Book of Common Prayer has helped to stimulate a renewed interest in its teaching and fundamental contribution to Anglican identity. Archbishop Cranmer and others involved in the English Reformation knew well that the content and shape of the services set out in the Prayer Book were vital ways of teaching congregations biblical truth and the principles of the Christian gospel. This basic idea of '*lex orandi, lex credendi*' is extremely important. For good or ill, the content and shape of our meetings as Christians is highly influential in shaping our practice in following the Lord Jesus Christ.

Furthermore, increased interest in the historic formularies of the Church of England has been generated by the current painful divisions within the Anglican Communion which inevitably highlight the matter of Anglican identity. In the end our Anglican Foundations cannot be avoided since our identity as Anglicans is intimately related to the question of Christian identity, and Christian identity cannot avoid questions of Christian understanding and belief. While the 39 Articles often become the focus of discussions about Christian and Anglican belief (and have been addressed in this series through *The Faith we Confess* by Gerald Bray) the fact that the 1662 Book of Common Prayer and the Ordinal are also part of the doctrinal foundations of the Church of England is often neglected.

Thus the aim of this series of booklets which focus on the Formularies of the Church of England and the elements of the services within the Prayer Book is to highlight what those services teach about the Christian faith and to demonstrate how they are also designed to shape the practice of that faith. As well as providing an account of the origins of the Prayer Book services, these booklets are designed to offer practical guidance on how such services may be used in Christian ministry nowadays.

It is not necessary to use the exact 1662 services in order to be true to our Anglican heritage, identity and formularies. However if we grasp the principles of Cranmer which underpinned those services then modern versions of them can fulfil the same task of teaching congregations how to live as Christians which Cranmer intended. If we are ignorant of the principles of Cranmer then our Sunday gatherings will inevitably teach something to Anglican congregations, but it will not be the robust biblical faith which Cranmer promoted.

So our hope is that through this Anglican Foundations series our identity as Anglicans will be clarified and that there will be by God's grace a renewal of the teaching and practice of the Christian faith through the services of the Church of England and elsewhere within the Anglican Communion.

Mark Burkill and Gerald Bray

Series Editors, The Latimer Trust

CONTENTS

Preface

I am grateful to the Latimer Trust for inviting me to write this booklet to commemorate the 350th anniversary of *The Book of Common Prayer*. When I joined my local Anglican church at the age of 12, I quickly embraced this Book, and grew to love its services. After I was converted to Christ at the age of 16, I grew to love its gospel truth, and the excellent expression of that truth in its prayers. The words of the BCP[1] still come naturally to my mind, and it continues to provide a standard by which I evaluate services I attend.

As I have written this booklet, my admiration for it has only increased, and I praise God for Thomas Cranmer and those other leaders of Reformed Anglicanism of the sixteenth and seventeenth centuries for the diligence, care, creativity and gospel faithfulness of their ministry in creating this Book.

The 1662 *Book of Common Prayer* remains a powerful instrument of ministry in the hand of God today. A couple came from England to Australia, and took up farming in the outback. They had both gone to their parish churches in England when young, but drifted away from church attendance. They were converted and nourished by their memories of the words of the General Confession of *The Book of Common Prayer*, and by the Thirty-Nine Articles, found in an old copy of the BCP, especially Article XI on Justification! Praise God for his mercy.

I am grateful to my colleagues and friends Rhys Bezzant, Wei-Han Kuan, and Mike Flynn for their productive feedback on an earlier draft of this work, and to Peter Williams and to the Latimer Trust for their practical help in producing this booklet.

Dedication

This booklet is dedicated to brothers and sisters in Christ within Anglicanism around the world who continue to hold to the gospel of Christ despite persecution and oppression.

---

[1]   The contraction 'BCP' will be used throughout to refer to the 1662 *Book of Common Prayer*

The 1662 *Book of Common Prayer* and 'the very pure Word of God' – a call to Biblical reformation

Learning from the past is a lost art for many, but it provides a rich resource for those who engage in it. It is easier to dismiss the past or to try to reproduce it: discerning and creative learning is more productive. 2012 is the three hundred and fiftieth anniversary of the publication of *The Book of Common Prayer* of 1662. It is a good opportunity for us to reflect on its significance.

We live in a society which has until recently had two contradictory tendencies: to discard the old and replace it with the most recent invention, or, to recover the old and present it without modernization. These two contradictory tendencies are found within our church life, where one tendency fuels the other. These tendencies are found in attitudes to the 1662 *Book of Common Prayer*,[1] which in fact includes three documents: *The Book of Common Prayer*, *The Articles of Religion*,[2] and *The Form and Manner of Making, Ordaining and Consecrating of Bishops, Priests and Deacons*.[3] Some have discarded it completely, and some claim to use it without change, even if in fact they use it with modifications. I do not think that we should use the 1662 Book universally today, and believe that to do so would compromise the intentions and integrity of the book. However I am also sure that we have much to learn from this Book, and that our Sunday services would be immeasurably enriched if we applied the principles and practices that it expresses. And many

---

[1] An electronic copy may be found at: http://www.churchofengland.org/prayer-worship/worship/book-of-common-prayer.aspx

[2] Books on the *Thirty-Nine Articles*: Gerald Bray, *The Faith We Confess*, (London: The Latimer Trust, 2009); D.B. Knox, *The Thirty-Nine Articles: The historic basis of Anglican Faith*, (London: Hodder and Stoughton, 1967); Oliver O'Donovan, *On the Thirty-Nine Articles: A Conversation with Tudor Christianity*, (Exeter: Paternoster Press, 1993); Ashley Null, *The Thirty-Nine Articles and Reformation Anglicanism*, (Mukono: Uganda Christian University, 2005); James I. Packer & Roger T. Beckwith, *The Thirty-Nine Articles: their Place and Use Today*, (2nd edition London: The Latimer Trust, 2006); W.H. Griffith Thomas, *The Principles of Theology: An Introduction to the Thirty-Nine Articles*, (Oregon: Wipf and Stock Publishers, 2005).

[3] See Martin Parsons, *The Ordinal: An Exposition of the Ordination Services*, The Prayer Book Commentaries, (London: Hodder and Stoughton, 1964).

young people have the enviable ability to enjoy the exotic past as well as the exciting present. Perhaps the BCP will have new life in the coming years!

I will also make use of *The Thirty-Nine Articles of Religion,* because the whole Book came as a package, and the doctrines of the Thirty-Nine Articles and the services in the rest of the Book are mutually explanatory and mutually illuminating. This version of the Articles was the one issued in 1571, which remained in force in 1662. I also make use of the *Book of Homilies,*[4] prescribed sermons commended in Article XXXV, and other writings of the Reformers. There are powerful resonances between the services of *The Book of Common Prayer*, its Prefaces, the *Articles of Religion*, and the *Homilies.*

1.1 Why consider the 1662 *Book of Common Prayer*?

There are three reasons why we should learn from 1662.

1.1.1 *The Book of Common Prayer was the product of a genuine attempt to reform and renew the Church of England.*

The Prayer Books of 1549, 1552, and 1662 were an attempt to express Biblical and Reformed Christianity in practice, and to teach and train people in that faith. They marked a massive reformation in the services of the church, to remove error, and to represent the truth. Those who hold to Biblical and Reformed Christianity should honour this attempt, and try to benefit from it. As we have much to learn from the theology of the Reformers, so we have much to learn from the changes they made in the church services. I hope to demonstrate the Biblical insights, the Reformed theology, and the pastoral wisdom that is evident in *The Book of Common Prayer*. The 1662 Book also models the value of retaining good things from the past. The reformers were consciously reforming the church, not starting a new church.

---

[4]   *Certain Homilies or Sermons appointed to be read in Churches in the time of Queen Elizabeth*, (London: SPCK, 1864).

1.1.2 *The identity of Anglicanism is still linked to The Book of Common Prayer*

While it is commonly claimed that Anglicans do not have doctrine, that is not the case. Canon A5 of the Church of England reads:

> The doctrine of the Church of England is grounded in the Holy Scriptures, and in such teachings of the Ancient Fathers and Councils of the Church as are agreeable to the said Scriptures.
>
> In particular such Doctrine is found in the Thirty-Nine Articles of Religion, The Book of Common Prayer, and the Ordinal.[5]

The same doctrinal identity is expressed in Canon C15, 'Of the Declaration of Assent':

> The Church of England is part of the One, Holy, Catholic and Apostolic Church worshipping the one true God, Father, Son and Holy Spirit. It professes the faith uniquely revealed in the Holy Scriptures and set forth in the catholic creeds, which faith the Church is called upon to proclaim afresh in each generation. Led by the Holy Spirit, it has borne witness to Christian truth in its historic formularies, the Thirty-Nine Articles of Religion, The Book of Common Prayer and the Ordering of Bishops, Priests and Deacons. In the declaration you are about to make will you affirm your loyalty to this inheritance of faith as your inspiration and guidance under God in bringing the grace and truth of Christ to this generation and making him known to those in your care?[6]

Stephen Sykes has noted that this is not just important for members of the Church of England, but also significant for all who claim to be Anglicans:

> The Book of Common Prayer, the Thirty-Nine Articles, and the Ordering of Bishops, Priests and Deacons....constitute what in the Church of England is spoken of as its "inheritance

---

[5] The Canons of the Church of England. http://www.churchofengland.org/about-us/structure/churchlawlegis/canons/canons-7th-edition.aspx

[6] The Canons.

of faith" (see Canon C15)...insofar as they define the faith inheritance of the See of Canterbury, and insofar as communion with that See defines what it means to belong to the Anglican Communion, these documents have significant authority among Anglicans throughout the world.[7]

We need to escape the tyranny of the present. If we follow the theory of our society that only the new is relevant and that the old is obsolete, we will also follow our society in divinising our deepest assumptions. These assumptions are invisible to us, because they are commonly held, and we live in a conformist society. These assumptions are like a submerged reef, ready to tear us apart. We tend to read them into the Bible, and so give them divine authority. We can learn so much from how other Biblical and Reformed Christians read the Bible in other cultures today, and we can learn so much from such Christians from the past. When we do this, we will easily see them practising their cultural assumptions in their lives and ministries, and this should be a warning that we are likely to do the same. But in addition, knowing what Christians have done in the past gives us a place to stand to evaluate our present, and to see our own assumptions more clearly, and so be better able to be free of them. Here is part of our family history: we understand ourselves better if we understand our past, and we may well learn good lessons from that past.

1.1.3   The 1662 Prayer Book is a vital clue to the Reformed identity of Anglicanism

While Luther's ideas had great impact on the Reformation in England, Swiss Reformed theology was influential from the 1530s, especially through Heinrich Bullinger, Martin Bucer, and Peter Martyr. Calvin's Reformed theology and practice became influential in the 1550s, with the translation of Calvin's *Institutes of the Christian Religion* and his sermons. It was expressed in the 1552

---

[7]   Stephen Sykes, 'The Anglican Character' in Ian Bunting, ed. *Celebrating the Anglican Way*, (London: Hodder and Stoughton, 1996), p. 23

Prayer Book under Edward VI.[8] It increased with the return of the Marian exiles from Geneva at the beginning of Elizabeth's reign.[9] Andrew Cinnamond wrote:

> Elizabethan theology therefore needs to be seen as another branch of international Reformed theology, very much in the vein of Calvin, Beza, Bucer, Bullinger and Peter Martyr.[10]

This Reformed tradition was strongly represented among the Bishops in the reign of James,[11] and continued under Charles I, despite the efforts of Archbishop Laud.[12] While Reformed theology was also present among the Baptists, the Brownists (Congregationalists) and Presbyterians in England, it also continued in the Church of England. Even when many Puritan Anglicans left in 1662, many remained and continued the Reformed tradition.[13] And despite the rise of Latitudinarianism and the High Church movement, it continued until it was re-energised in the Evangelical Revival, especially under

---

[8] Dairmaid MacCulloch, *Building a Godly Realm: The Establishment of English Protestantism*, (London: The Historical Association, 1992); and Dairmaid MacCulloch, *The Boy King: Edward VI and the Protestant Reformation*, (New York: Palgrave, 1999).

[9] Peter Lake, *Moderate Puritans and the Elizabethan Church*, (Cambridge: Cambridge University Press, 1982).

[10] Andrew Cinnamond, *What Matters in Reforming the Church? Puritan Grievances under Elizabeth I*, St Antholin Lectureship, (London: The Latimer Trust, 2011), p. 2.

[11] Kenneth Fincham, *Prelate as Pastor: the Episcopate of James I*, (Oxford: Oxford University Press, 1990); and Kenneth Fincham, *The Early Stuart Church 1603-1642*, (Stanford: Stanford University Press, 1993).

[12] David W. Doerksen, *Conforming to the Word: Herbert, Donne, and the English Church before Laud*, (Lewisburg: Bucknell University Press/London: Associated University Presses, 1997); Mary Arshagouni Papazian, *John Donne and the Protestant Reformation: New Perspectives*, (Detroit: Wayne State University Press, 2003); Julian Davies, *The Caroline captivity of the church: Charles I and the remoulding of Anglicanism 1625-1641*, (Oxford: Clarendon Press, 1992); Frank Livingstone Huntley, *Bishop Joseph Hall 1574-1656*, (Cambridge: DS Brewer, 1979); Isabel M. Calder, *Activities of the Puritan Faction of the Church of England 1625-33*, (London: SPCK, 1957); and Tom Webster, *Godly Clergy in Early Stuart England: The Caroline Puritan Movement c1620-1643*, (Cambridge: Cambridge University Press, 1997).

[13] Stephen Hampton, *Anti-Arminians: The Anglican Reformed Tradition from Charles II to George I*, (Oxford: Oxford University Press, 2008).

leaders like George Whitfield and Augustus Toplady.[14] So it continued until today, with renewed energy in the 19th Century, and again after the Second World War in the 20th Century.[15] We also see its great influence within international Anglicanism.

I realise that at least two groups of people prefer the theory that Puritans cannot be Anglicans, nor can Anglicans be Puritans.[16] Some Non-Conformists may take this view because they want to emphasise the gulf between Anglicanism and Puritanism, to show that true Puritanism is found outside Anglicanism. Some Anglican writers take this view because they want to claim that Puritanism has no place in mainstream Anglicanism.

However Patrick Collinson has shown that Puritanism was part of Anglicanism: 'our modern conception (that) Anglicanism commonly excludes puritanism is ... a distortion of part of our religious history'.[17] A.G. Dickens claimed that:

> Puritanism in our sense was never limited to Nonconformists; it was a powerful element in the origins of the Anglican Church and it was through that Church that it won its abiding role in the life and outlook of the nation.[18]

The leaders of Puritan Anglicans included: Archbishop Grindal of Canterbury, who tried to defend Puritan training of preachers against Queen Elizabeth;[19] Archbishop Williams of York, author of *The Holy Table, Name and Thing*, a sturdy defence of the Reformed theology

---

[14] Lee Gatiss, *The True Profession of the Gospel: Augustus Toplady and reclaiming our Reformed foundations*, (London: The Latimer Trust, 2010).

[15] Kenneth Hylson-Smith, *Evangelicals in the Church of England, 1734-1984*, (Edinburgh: T&T Clark, 1989); Randle Manwaring, *From Controversy to Co-existence: Evangelicals in the Church of England 1914-1980*, (Cambridge: Cambridge University Press, 1985), and Richard Turnbull, *Anglican and Evangelical?* (London: Continuum, 2007).

[16] I have also expressed these ideas in Peter Adam, 'A Church "Halfly Reformed": the Puritan Dilemma' republished in Lee Gatiss, ed., *Pilgrims, Warriors, and Servants, The St Antholin's Lectures, Volume 1, 1991-200*, (London: The Latimer Trust, 2010).

[17] Patrick Collinson, *The Elizabethan Puritan Movement*, (London: Jonathan Cape, 1967), p. 467.

[18] A.G. Dickens, *The English Reformation*, (London: Collins, 1967), p. 428.

[19] Patrick Collinson, *Archbishop Grindal 1519-1583: The Struggle for a Reformed Church*, (London: Jonathan Cape, 1979).

and practice of the Lord's Supper;[20] and Archbishop Ussher of Armagh, who together with Richard Baxter promoted a Reformed model of Primitive Episcopacy.[21] Nigel Atkinson has shown that Richard Hooker, a great architect of Anglicanism, was clearly in the Reformed tradition, and was closer to Calvin in theology than some of his Puritan critics.[22] Even in the days of the Commonwealth, 300 Episcopal Puritans (called 'Evangelicals' by a contemporary writer) used to meet regularly in Oxford for Anglican worship.[23] Paul Zahl points out that the English Reformation lasted 170 years, from 1520 to 1690, and resulted in 'a Protestant Reformed Church and a Protestant Reformed nation'.[24] Many now recognize that the Church of England from Edward VI to Charles I was, in the memorable words of Dewey Wallace, 'a Reformed church with hankerings after Lutheranism'.[25] The 1662 *Book of Common Prayer* was the product of one hundred and fifty years of reformation, and is an important historical sign of the Reformed identity of Anglicanism.

Here are three good reasons to study and learn from *The Book of Common Prayer*. However before we do this, it is worthwhile to understand some particular contexts of the 1662 Book, which will help us make sense of some features of it.

---

[20] John Williams, *The Work of Archbishop John Williams*, ed. Barrie Williams, (Abingdon: Sutton Courtenay Press, 1980).

[21] Alan Ford, *James Ussher: theology, history and politics in early-modern Ireland and England*, (Oxford: OUP, 2007); Crawford Gribben, *The Irish Puritans: James Ussher and the Reformation of the Church*, (Darlington: Evangelical Press, 2003); and Wallace Benn, 'Ussher on Bishops: A Reforming ecclesiology', reprinted in Lee Gatiss, ed. *Preachers, Pastors, Ambassadors: Puritan Wisdom for Today's Church, St Antholin's Lectures, Volume 2, 2001-2010* (London: The Latimer Trust, 2011), pp. 97-122.

[22] Nigel Atkinson, *Richard Hooker and the Authority of Scripture, Tradition and Reason*, (Carlisle: Paternoster, 1997).

[23] V.H.H. Green, *Religion at Oxford and Cambridge*, (London: SCM, 1964), p. 147.

[24] Paul F.M. Zahl, *The Protestant Face of Anglicanism*, (Grand Rapids/Cambridge: Eerdmans, 1998), p. 27.

[25] As quoted in Zahl, *Protestant Face*, p. 15. See also Nicholas Tyacke, *Aspects of English Protestantism, c.1530-1700*, (Manchester: Manchester University Press, 2001); and David Samuel, ed., *The Evangelical Succession in the Church of England*, (Cambridge: James Clarke, 1979).

1.2   The particular contexts of the *Book of Common Prayer*

The 1662 *Book of Common Prayer* was the result of a long process of reform, including the English Prayer Books that preceded it, beginning in 1549.

1.2.1   *The BCP was the product of the political English Reformation*

The English Reformation was the product of a distinctive mixture of politics and religion. The politics included the rise of nationalism in Europe which brought with it the desire for national churches; Henry VIII's plan to divorce his wife Katharine of Aragon which led him to remove the Church of England from the power of the Pope; and Henry's desire to take over the property of the monasteries. The political implications of the religious affiliations of Henry's successors were important, including the Reformed theology of Edward, Mary's Roman Catholicism, the moderate Protestantism of Elizabeth and James, the rise of more High-church Arminianism under Charles I, the rise and fall of the Congregationalist and Presbyterian Commonwealth, and the Restoration of the monarchy in Charles II in 1660. The political context of England also led to a fear of Roman Catholics, both in other countries (France and Spain), and also within England.

1.2.2   *The BCP was a product of the religious English Reformation*

This Reformation gained its distinctive character from the earlier Bible teaching ministry of Wycliffe and the Lollards, and William Tyndale's sacrificial work in Bible translation. It was influenced by the Continental Reformation, initially by the writings of Martin Luther and the Swiss Reformation, and then by those of John Calvin. Calvin's influence was reinforced by those refugees from Mary who fled to Geneva, and later returned to England. The English Reformation was also the product of those Puritan members of the Church of England who wished for further Reformation,[26] as well as by the rise of the Baptists, the Brownists (Congregationalists), and the Presbyterians. It was influenced by the Arminian and High Church

---

[26]   Adam, 'Halfly Reformed', pp. 185-216.

9

movement during the reign of Charles I, which was also present in the reign of Charles II. It was also influenced by reaction against the Quakers,[27] and the continuing presence of Roman Catholics.

1.2.3 The BCP was the product of the work of Archbishop Cranmer

It was Cranmer who reworked older sources to produce the Reformed Prayer Books of 1549 and 1552. He made a remarkable contribution to the expression of Reformed Anglicanism in the services that he devised, the prayers that he wrote, and in the prayer books that he compiled.[28] The Prayer Book of 1662 was based on his book of 1552. His 1549 book was the first attempt to provide a Reformed prayer book. His book of 1552 was even more Reformed in theology and practice. This book was abandoned under Mary, and then reinstituted in a slightly modified form under Elizabeth in 1559. That book continued to be used under James and Charles I, and was then reissued in a modified form as *The Book of Common Prayer* under Charles II in 1662. So Archbishop Cranmer's 1552 Prayer Book formed the basis of our 1662 Book. As William Tyndale's translation of the Bible formed the basis for subsequent translations including the 1611 Authorised Version, so Cranmer's 1552 Book formed the basis of the 1662 *Book of Common Prayer*.

1.2.4 The BCP was a book for a National Church

With the reforms of Henry VIII, the power of the Pope had been replaced by the power of the King, supplemented by the power of Parliament. So the Church had a national identity, and successive monarchs wanted the unity and cohesion of the Church to serve the

---

[27] Peter Adam, 'Word and Spirit: the Puritan-Quaker Debate', republished in Gatiss, (ed.), *Preachers, Pastors, Ambassadors*, pp. 49-96.

[28] In Dairmaid MacCulloch, *Thomas Cranmer: A Life*, (New Haven and London: Yale University Press, 1996), see pp. 173-236, for the Swiss Reformed influence on Cranmer in the 1530s, pp. 454-513 for the progress of Reformed theology and practice in 1550-52, and pp. 614-617 for his Reformed view of the Lord's Supper. See further, Philip Edgcumbe Hughes, *Theology of the English Reformers*, (London: Hodder and Stoughton, 1965), pp. 141-158; and Ashley Null, 'Thomas Cranmer and Tudor Evangelicalism', in Michael A.G. Haykin and Kenneth J. Stewart, eds., *The Emergence of Evangelicalism: Exploring Historical Continuities*, (Nottingham: Apollos, 2008), pp. 221-251.

political unity of the nation. The Tudor monarchy was very authoritarian, and we see that reflected in the Church of England of their days, and so in the Prayer Books that they imposed. On the one hand this had the effect of marginalizing Roman Catholics (except of course during the reign of Mary), and on the other hand, of marginalizing Protestants who did not agree with the enforced details of various monarchs' models of the Reformation. As it was a book for a National Church, it imposed one pattern for services, in place of the various patterns previously in use.[29] It was intended to serve the political unity of the nation, by imposing a religious unity.

1.2.5 *The BCP was a book with great expectations of the local parish church*

The dissolution of the monasteries by Henry VIII had a profound effect on the Church in England. In the pre-Reformation era, monasteries were para-church ministries that were established to provide well-resourced and high level education, training, evangelism, Bible teaching, social care, and worship. They vastly overshadowed the parishes in their resources and the quality of their ministry. With the closure of the monasteries, some education and training was taken over by the Universities, and by newly founded local Grammar Schools. There were new demands on parishes to provide daily prayers, education and preaching, social care, and community cohesion. So the life of prayer formerly provided by the monasteries was now to be provided by parishes. The formal preaching provided by monasteries and the popular preaching provided by the Preaching Orders was now provided by parishes. Similarly, the role of social care also moved from monasteries to parishes. *The Book of Common Prayer* marked the raising of the expectation for ordinary Christians attending their local church in terms of daily prayer, Bible knowledge, intercession, understanding, and Christian lifestyle, as it also raised expectations of parish clergy. Whereas formerly there had been two standards, the higher for the

---

[29] 'And whereas heretofore there hath been great diversity in saying and singing in Churches within this Realm; some following Salisbury Use, some Hereford Use, and some the Use of Bangor, some of York, some of Lincoln; now from henceforth all the whole Realm shall have but one Use'. BCP, 'Concerning the Service of the Church'.

monk and nuns, and the lower for parish clergy and lay people, now there was one standard, and much more was expected of both parish clergy and lay people. The 1662 Book represented that higher standard.

1.2.6 *The BCP was a book for a different age*

It was a book for a Nation: in our age we are likely to expect our intercessions and prayers to be more open to local issues. It was a book from a Monarchist age: if we have Monarchs, they are now constitutional agents, subject to Parliament. It has set forms of service and readings: we are likely to feel that local initiative and variation is more attractive. It has set prayers: we may feel that spontaneous prayers are of higher spiritual value. It has a structured and formal style: we may think that spontaneity, variety, and creativity provide a better style today. Its English is dated in style: we rightly feel that we should speak the language of our age. But these characteristics which may make us feel that it is a distant book should not blind us to its value. Of course we should find styles and patterns which match our own cultural context; though we should also be wary of assuming that our own cultural assumptions are spiritually superior to those of a former age.[30]

1.3 *The purpose of this booklet*

This booklet focuses on one aspect of that Book, its deep and wide commitment to the Bible, and its commitment to 'the very pure Word of God'.[31] I am writing with two audiences in mind: those who do not identify with the Reformed identity and practice of Anglicanism, and those who do.

So, for those who do not identify with the Reformed identity and practice of Anglicanism, I want them to learn from the 1662 Book how they might recover that identity and practice. Michael Ramsey, Archbishop of Canterbury, wrote of the constant need for

---

[30] There is no Biblical evidence to support the view that informality is more spiritual than informality, or that spontaneous prayers are more spiritual than prepared prayers. These ideas come from our culture, not from the Bible. And we sing some songs repeatedly!

[31] BCP, 'Concerning the Service'.

the Anglican Church to relearn the Gospel, and to test itself by the standards of the Reformation:

> The full recovery of the doctrine of the Church is bound up with the return of the Gospel of God. Catholicism, created by the Gospel, finds its power in terms of the Gospel alone. Neither the massive polity of the Church, nor its devotional life, nor its traditions in order and worship can in themselves serve to define Catholicism; for all these things have their meaning in the Gospel, wherein the true definition of Catholicism is found.[32]

And again:

> 'The Word of God', 'sola fide', 'sola gratia', 'soli Deo gloria'... are Catholicism's own themes, and out of them it was born. But they are themes learnt and re-learnt in humiliation, and Catholicism always stands before the church door at Wittenberg to read the truth by which she is created and by which also she is judged.[33]

To which I would add that in addition to a visit to Wittenberg to read Martin Luther, a visit to Geneva to hear John Calvin would also help, and, perhaps more to the point, a visit to the Reformed doctrine and practice of the 1662 *Book of Common Prayer* with its adherence to 'the very pure Word of God'. Ramsey also criticized the Liberal Catholics of the Church of England, because:

> in their intense concentration upon the Incarnation as the key to the understanding of the world, these writers and their subsequent followers were minimizing the Cross, the divine judgement and the eschatological element in the Gospel.[34]

---

[32] A.M. Ramsey, *The Gospel and the Catholic Church*, (London: Longmans, Green, 1956), p. 179.

[33] Ramsey, *The Gospel*, p. 180.

[34] A.M. Ramsey, *From Gore to Temple: The Development of Anglican Theology between Lux Mundi and the Second World War 1889-1939*, (London: Longmans, 1960), p. 9.

Again, revisiting the 1662 *Book of Common Prayer* would help. It aimed to express what the Act of Uniformity of 1662 described as 'the reformed religion of the Church of England'.[35]

This booklet is also written for those who value the Biblical and Reformed identity and practice of Anglicanism, but who do not use the BCP, and may be reluctant to use any prayer book. I think that they too have much to learn from that Book, especially its comprehensive and effective use of the Bible. A visit to *The Book of Common Prayer* would benefit those who value the Biblical, Reformed and Evangelical heritage of Anglicanism. Those who claim to be Biblical might well learn useful lessons from the intentional and comprehensive Biblicism of *The Book of Common Prayer*. John Wesley wrote:

> I believe there is no Liturgy in the world, either in ancient or modern language, which breathes more of a solid, scriptural, rational piety than the Common Prayer of the Church of England.[36]

The nineteenth Century Evangelical leader Charles Simeon preached 'On the Excellency of the Liturgy' (that is, *The Book of Common Prayer*), and had a high estimation of the value that Book. He claimed:

> The finest sight short of heaven would be a whole congregation using the prayers of the Liturgy in the true spirit of them.[37]

Although he famously valued the ministry of preaching, he also valued his 'reading-desk', from which he led the congregation in prayer: 'Never do I find myself nearer to God than often I am in the

[35] 1662 Act of Uniformity, as quoted in Gerald Bray, ed., *Documents of the English Reformation*, (Minneapolis: Fortress Press, 1994), p. 548.
[36] From the preface to *John Wesley's Prayer Book: The Sunday Service of the Methodists in North America* (James F. White, ed.; Cleveland: OSL Publications, 1991).
[37] Hugh Evan Hopkins, *Charles Simeon of Cambridge*, (London: Hodder and Stoughton, 1977), pp. 42,43.

reading-desk'.[38] He recognized the practical superiority of 'precomposed' prayers:

> If all men could pray at all times as some men can sometimes, then indeed we might prefer extempore to precomposed prayers.[39]

After a visit to Scotland, and the experience of much extempore prayer, he commented: 'Thank God we have a Liturgy'.[40]

Perhaps we have lost more than we realise in dispensing with the BCP, and in our reluctance to use 'precomposed' prayers and services.

---

[38]   Hopkins, *Simeon*, p. 42.
[39]   Hopkins, *Simeon*, p. 213.
[40]   Hopkins, *Simeon*, p. 190.

2 What can we learn from the 1662 Book?

The Book of Common Prayer is richly and deeply Biblical, and still provides a standard that challenges and enriches us. Its aim was that:

> nothing is ordained to be read, but the very pure Word of God, the holy Scriptures, or that which is agreeable to the same.[1]

There are four dynamics that makes it a comprehensively Biblical Book:

- It is intentionally formed by Biblical truth, and focused on the gospel of Christ.

- It precludes and corrects un-Biblical and anti-Biblical doctrines and practices.

- The Bible is to be both read and preached, and is the chief instrument of ministry.

- It provides responses to God that express Bible truths and use Bible words.

2.1 *The Book of Common Prayer is intentionally formed by Biblical truth, and focused on the gospel of Christ.*

2.1.1 *It is formed by Biblical truth*

We read in 1 Timothy that God's people are 'the church of the living God, the pillar and bulwark of the truth', (1 Timothy 3:15), and in his great prayer for his people before he died, Christ prayed to his heavenly Father, 'sanctify them in the truth, your word is truth' (John 17:17).

Canon A5 of the Church England informs us that 'The doctrine of the Church of England is grounded in the Holy Scriptures...' and this principle endorses the priority of *The Book of Common Prayer*. So the Preface to the 1662 Book includes the following claim:

---

[1]   BCP, 'Concerning the Service'.

16

> For we are fully persuaded in our judgements (and we here profess it to the world) that the Book, as it stood before established by Law, doth not contain in it any thing contrary to the Word of God, or to sound Doctrine, or which a godly man may not with a good Conscience use and submit unto, or which is not fairly defensible against any that shall oppose the same.

Article VI of the Thirty-*Nine Articles* claims the sufficiency of Scripture for salvation:

> Holy Scripture containeth all things necessary to salvation: so that whatsoever is not read therein, nor may be proved thereby, is not to be required of any man, that it should be believed as an article of the Faith, or be thought requisite or necessary to salvation.

The effect of this is to prohibit non-Biblical ideas being taught as part of the Christian Faith, or necessary for salvation. So there is no idea that tradition or reason may have equal authority to that of Scripture.[2] Indeed Article VIII accepts the Creeds on the basis of their Scriptural content:

> The Three Creeds, Nicene Creed, Athanasius's Creed, and that which is commonly called the Apostles' Creed, ought thoroughly to be received and believed: for they may be proved by most certain warrants of holy Scripture.

We may think that the Book did not in fact succeed in being 'merely Biblical'. But that was its intention and purpose. Its aim was to represent the fullness of the Biblical revelation, but not to go beyond that revelation. And Bishop John Jewel wrote of the power of Scripture:

> It is the Word of God: God openeth His mouth and speaketh to us, to guide us into all truth, to make us full and ready in all good works, that we may be perfect men in Christ Jesus; so

---

[2] There is no evidence in *The Book of Common Prayer* to support the frequent claim of the 'Three-fold cord' of Scripture, Tradition and Reason as classic Anglicanism. Tradition is valued if it is supported by Scripture, and dismissed if it is not. There is no evidence in the BCP to support the idea that Reason is a reliable source of theology.

that, rooted and grounded in him, that we may not be tossed to and fro with every tempest.[3]

2.1.2   *The focus is on the gospel of Christ*

The gospel is central to the identity, life, and mission of the church:

> For there is one God; there is also one mediator between God and humankind, Christ Jesus, himself human, who gave himself a ransom for all (1 Timothy 2:5,6).

The central gospel message of the Bible is communicated in the BCP in a variety of ways. There is a constant restating of the gospel, of salvation history, and of Biblical theology.

The daily repetition of the Psalms reminds us of God the creator and sustainer of the universe, the creation of his people, his covenants of love, his rescue as their deliverer, his answers to their prayers, his forgiveness of their sins, and his call to them to trust and obey him. For the book of Psalms is the Bible in miniature. As Martin Luther wrote:

> (The Book of Psalms) should be precious and dear to us if only because it most clearly promises the death and resurrection of Christ, and describes His kingdom, and the nature and standing of all Christian people. It could well be called a 'little Bible' since it contains, set out in the briefest and most beautiful form, all that is to be found in the whole Bible...[4]

The shape of Morning and Evening Prayer is a reminder of the gospel. Both services begin with the word of God in a quotation from the Bible, such as 'When the wicked man turneth away from his wickedness that he hath committed, and doeth that which is lawful and right, he shall save his soul alive. *Ezek.* xviii. 27'. How wonderful to start a service with God's words of gospel invitation!

---

[3]   As quoted in Hughes, *Theology*, p. 39, from John Jewel, *The Works of Bishop Jewel*, ed. John Ayer, Vol IV, (Cambridge: The University Press, 1850), p. 1166. See further, Hughes, *Theology*, pp. 9-53.

[4]   Martin Luther, Preface to Psalms, in John Dillenberger, ed, *Martin Luther: Selections from his writings*, (New York: Anchor Books, 1961), p. 38.

The congregation is then summoned to turn to God and repent of their sin in words which remind them of the purpose of their meeting:

> Dearly beloved brethren, the Scripture moveth us, in sundry places, to acknowledge and confess our manifold sins and wickedness; and that we should not dissemble nor cloak them before the face of Almighty God our heavenly Father; but confess them with an humble, lowly, penitent, and obedient heart; to the end that we may obtain forgiveness of the same, by his infinite goodness and mercy. And although we ought, at all times, humbly to acknowledge our sins before God; yet ought we chiefly so to do, when we assemble and meet together to render thanks for the great benefits that we have received at his hands, to set forth his most worthy praise, to hear his most holy Word, and to ask those things which are requisite and necessary, as well for the body as the soul...[5]

The congregation then confesses their sin, and is assured of God's forgiveness.[6]

They then respond to God in the words of the Psalms. The recitation of the Psalms in the vernacular is a common sign of Reformation faith. Luther encouraged the singing of the Psalms, as did Calvin and the Swiss Reformation. Metrical Psalms were popular among Presbyterians, and were introduced to the Church of England with the settings of Sternhold and Hopkins from 1547, and Tate and Brady from 1690.

Calvin wrote that the Book of Psalms was 'an anatomy of all parts of the soul'.[7] So the daily recitation of the Psalms provides an opportunity for us to know God and to know ourselves, and to meditate and reflect on our life before God.

Each Psalm concludes with the words:

---

[5]   Notice that the word 'worship' is missing from this statement of the purpose of meeting!

[6]   I would have included more of the atoning death of Christ in the Absolution!

[7]   John Calvin, Preface to the Psalms, in *Commentaries on The Book of Joshua and the Psalms of David and others*, Calvin Translation Society, Vol. IV, (Reprinted, Grand Rapids: Baker, 1981), p. xxxvii.

Glory be to the Father, and to the Son: and to the Holy Ghost; As it was in the beginning, is now, and ever shall be: world without end. Amen.

These words call for God the Holy Trinity to be praised, and give the theological context of the Psalms and the readings from the Bible.

The Bible is then read, one reading from the Old Testament and one reading from the New Testament. The congregation joins in a canticle in response to each reading, and the canticles themselves provide a summary of God's character and his saving work, for example in the Song of Zechariah, the Te Deum, the Magnificat, and the Song of Simeon.

The congregation then responds to the word of God with an affirmation of their faith in God revealed in the reading of Scriptures, with the words of the Creed, that great summary of faith in God the Trinity and the person and work of Christ.

The congregation then brings their prayers and intercessions to God with prayers that show their responsibility for nation and church, and remind them of their daily duty of service to God in the world. The 1662 service then ends with these words, which are the Trinitarian gospel in miniature:

The grace of our Lord Jesus Christ, and the love of God, and the fellowship of the Holy Ghost, be with us all evermore (2 Corinthians 13:14).

And, for much of Anglican history since 1662, they then hear a sermon, and also sing hymns and songs during the whole service.[8]

It is a sad commentary on modern Anglicanism that even cathedrals and college chapels which promise services according to

---

[8]   The 1662 services of Morning and Evening Prayer do not make provision for a sermon. The sermon was to be preached at Holy Communion, and the expectation was that the congregation would attend Morning Prayer, Holy Communion, and Evening Prayer each Sunday. When Morning and Evening Prayer dominated over Holy Communion, sermons were added to those services, though many clergy removed their surplices and preached in an academic gown, to mark the fact that the formal service had ended. Hymns and songs for the congregation to sing were first introduced in the form of metrical psalms. Hymns and songs that were not limited to the words of Scripture were introduced by the Evangelical Revival.

The Book of Common Prayer so often produce Evensong and omit the gospel beginning to the service of Evening Prayer, including the confession of sin and the absolution. This is a sad fall from the Reformed theology of the BCP.

Participation in these services every day or every week provides a constant reminder of the need to turn to God the Saviour through Christ for the forgiveness of sins, to hear and obey the Scriptures, to believe in God the Trinity, and to pray to him for his mercy. Being trained to pray gospel prayers must bear gospel fruit. The services of Morning and Evening Prayer are designed to convert by immersing people in the truths of the Biblical gospel.

The gospel is strongly rehearsed in the service of Holy Communion, not least in the 'Comfortable Words':

> This is a true saying, and worthy of all men to be received, That Christ Jesus came into the world to save sinners. If any man sin, we have an Advocate with the Father, Jesus Christ the righteous; and he is the propitiation for our sins.[9]

It is also rehearsed in the Prayer of Consecration:

> Almighty God, our heavenly Father, who of thy tender mercy didst give thine only Son Jesus Christ to suffer death upon the Cross for our redemption; who made there (by his one oblation of himself once offered) a full, perfect, and sufficient sacrifice, oblation, and satisfaction, for the sins of the whole world...[10]

As the 20th Century liturgical scholar Dom Gregory Dix observed, this service of Holy Communion was 'the only effective attempt ever made to give liturgical expression to the doctrine of "justification by faith alone"'.[11]

Gospel assurance lies in the finished work of Christ, and the certain work of God in applying the benefits of the saving work of Christ to our lives, promised in the Scriptures, and received by faith. We find these themes in the Articles:

---

[9]   BCP, 'Holy Communion'.
[10]   BCP, 'Holy Communion'.
[11]   Gregory Dix, *The Shape of the Liturgy*, (London: Dacre Press, 1945), p. 672.

The Offering of Christ once made is that perfect redemption, propitiation, and satisfaction, for all the sins of the whole world, both original and actual; and there is none other satisfaction for sin, but that alone...[12]

We are accounted righteous before God, only for the merit of our Lord and Saviour Jesus Christ by Faith, and not for our own works or deservings: Wherefore, that we are justified by Faith only is a most wholesome Doctrine, and very full of comfort, as more largely is expressed in the Homily of Justification.[13]

Predestination to Life is the everlasting purpose of God, whereby (before the foundations of the world were laid) he hath constantly decreed by his counsel secret to us, to deliver from curse and damnation those whom he hath chosen in Christ out of mankind, and to bring them by Christ to everlasting salvation, as vessels made to honour. Wherefore, they which be endued with so excellent a benefit of God be called according to God's purpose by his Spirit working in due season: they through Grace obey the calling: they be justified freely: they be made sons of God by adoption: they be made like the image of his only-begotten Son Jesus Christ: they walk religiously in good works, and at length, by God's mercy, they attain to everlasting felicity...Furthermore, we must receive God's promises in such wise, as they be generally set forth to us in holy Scripture: and, in our doings, that Will of God is to be followed, which we have expressly declared unto us in the Word of God.[14]

We would do well to ensure that all the prayers we pray, all the words we say, and all the words we sing express Biblical faith and the gospel of Christ.

That is not to say that we only speak words that come from the Bible! But we do need work on teaching people Biblical language and vocabulary and perspectives, and helping them to learn to use

---

[12]   Thirty-Nine Articles, Article XXXI, 'Of the one Oblation of Christ finished upon the Cross'.

[13]   Thirty-Nine Articles, Article XI, 'Of the Justification of Man'.

[14]   Thirty-Nine Articles, Article XVII, 'Of Predestination and Election'.

these in their own response to God. And we should certainly ensure that all the words we use express the doctrines of the Bible, and do not distort or contradict them. The Reformers followed this policy with rigour. We should follow their example.

2.2 *The Book of Common Prayer precludes and corrects un-Biblical and anti-Biblical doctrines and practices.*

2.2.1 *It distinguishes between Biblical doctrines and other doctrines*

Jesus Christ warned the religious leaders of his day, 'You abandon the commandment of God and hold to human tradition' (Mark 7:8). St Jude wrote to the church, 'I appeal to you to contend for the faith that was once for all entrusted to the saints' (Jude 3).

Articles XX and XXI, on the authority of the Church and the authority of General Councils, make it clear that both Church and Councils are subservient to the Bible:

> The Church hath power to decree Rites or Ceremonies, and authority in Controversies of Faith: And yet it is not lawful for the Church to ordain anything contrary to God's Word written, neither may it so expound one place of Scripture, that it be repugnant to another. Wherefore, although the Church be a witness and a keeper of holy Writ, yet, as it ought not to decree any thing against the same, so besides the same ought it not to enforce any thing to be believed for necessity of Salvation.

> General Councils may not be gathered together without the commandment and will of Princes. And when they be gathered together, (forasmuch as they be an assembly of men, whereof all be not governed with the Spirit and Word of God,) they may err, and sometimes have erred, even in things pertaining unto God. Wherefore things ordained by them as necessary to salvation have neither strength nor authority, unless it may be declared that they be taken out of holy Scripture.

This was a characteristic stance of the Reformation, to place the Bible above the Church, its General Councils, and, of course, the Pope. It reflects the stance expressed by Cranmer:

My very foundation is only upon God's Word, which foundation is so sure that it never will fail.[15]

If there were any word of God beside the Scripture, we could never be certain of God's Word; and if we be uncertain of God's Word the devil might bring in among us new word, a new doctrine, a new faith, a new church, a new, God, or even himself to be god...If the Church and the Christian faith did not stay itself upon the word of God certain, as upon a sure and strong foundation, no man could know where he had the right faith, and whether he were in the true Church of Christ, or in the synagogue of Satan.[16]

For it is not enough to decide to be Biblical, if we do not also decide to preclude non-Biblical or anti-Biblical content. This is a decision about the doctrine of the Bible, not about sources. Only doctrine expressed and supported by the Bible is to be allowed, and doctrines that opposed or deflected attention from the Bible doctrines are forbidden. It is not about sources, for 1662 included material from sources outside the Bible, such as the Creeds, Canticles and hymns, like the 'Te Deum' and 'Come Holy Ghost'. But they selected material that expressed Biblical doctrine, in the same way that we choose hymns and songs and we pray using material that does not come directly from the Bible but which expresses Biblical doctrine.

This same doctrinal exclusivism is expressed in the Homily, 'The Reading of Holy Scripture':

Let us diligently search for the well of life in the books of the New and Old Testament, and not run to the stinking puddles of men's traditions... Nothing more darkeneth Christ and the glory of God, nor bringeth in more blindness and all kinds of

---

[15] Thomas Cranmer, *Writing and Disputations of Thomas Cranmer...Relative to the Sacrament of the Lord's Supper*, The Parker Society, ed. J.E. Cox, (Cambridge: The University Press, 1844), p. 255.

[16] Thomas Cranmer, *Miscellaneous Writings and Letters of Thomas Cranmer*, The Parker Society, ed. J.E. Cox, (Cambridge: The University Press, 1846), p. 52. (From the *Confutation of Unwritten Verities*, which may be by Cranmer, and certainly contains some of his work).

vices, than doth the ignorance of God's word.[17]

This same principle is enunciated in one of the prefaces to *The Book of Common Prayer*, which applies it to what is read in Church, namely, 'the very pure Word of God...or what is agreeable to the same':

> So that here you have an Order for Prayer, and for the reading of the holy Scripture, much agreeable to the mind and purpose of the old Fathers, and a great deal more profitable and commodious, than that which of late was used. It is more profitable, because here are left out many things, whereof some are untrue, some uncertain, some vain and superstitious; and nothing is ordained to be read, but the very pure Word of God, the holy Scriptures, or that which is agreeable to the same...[18]

Exclusivism is fundamental to Christianity. In the Ten Commandments, we meet the one who said, 'I am the LORD your God', and who added, 'you shall have no other gods before me' (Exodus 20:2-3). Jesus Christ told us, 'I am the way, and the truth, and the life', and added, 'No one comes to the Father except through me' (John 14:6). Paul wrote of the elder or bishop:

> He must have a firm grasp of the word that is trustworthy in accordance with the teaching, so that he may be able both to preach with sound doctrine and to refute those who contradict it (Titus 1:9).

Exclusivism requires following what is the only truth, and forbidding contrary ideas and loyalties. As Christ taught, 'Whoever is not with me is against me, and whoever does not gather with me scatters' (Matthew 12:30).

2.2.2 *It ensures that the actions and ceremonies express Biblical truth*

There were two kinds of actions and ceremonies to consider. The first were the sacraments, and the second other actions and ceremonies.

---

[17] *The First Book of Homilies*, 'A fruitful exhortation to the Reading of Holy Scripure', (first part), p. 2.
[18] BCP, 'Concerning the Service'.

The Roman Catholic Church had seven sacraments: Baptism, the Mass, Ordination, Matrimony, Confirmation, Absolution, and Extreme Unction. The reformed Anglican Church accepted only two Christ-ordained sacraments:

> There are two Sacraments ordained of Christ our Lord in the Gospel, that is to say, Baptism, and the Supper of the Lord. Those five commonly called Sacraments, that is to say, Confirmation, Penance, Orders, Matrimony, and extreme Unction, are not to be counted for Sacraments of the Gospel, being such as have grown partly of the corrupt following of the Apostles, partly are states of life allowed in the Scriptures; but yet have not like nature of Sacraments with Baptism, and the Lord's Supper, for that they have not any visible sign or ceremony ordained of God...[19]

They held that the two gospel sacraments were shaped by the gospel: that is, they were fundamentally about the work of God applied in our lives:

> Sacraments ordained of Christ be not only badges or tokens of Christian men's profession, but rather they be certain sure witnesses, and effectual signs of grace, and God's good will towards us, by the which he doth work invisibly in us, and doth not only quicken, but also strengthen and confirm our Faith in him.[20]

And they held that, although it was permitted to do actions in church that were not commanded by Christ, such as Marriage, Funerals, Ordination and Morning and Evening Prayer, etc, Christ's sacraments should be celebrated as he commanded, with no additions or subtractions:

> The Sacraments were not ordained of Christ to be gazed upon, or to be carried about, but that we should duly use them.[21]

The Sacrament of the Lord's Supper was not by Christ's

---

[19] Thirty-Nine Articles, Article XXV, 'Of the Sacraments'.
[20] Thirty-Nine Articles, Article XXV, 'Of the Sacraments'.
[21] Thirty-Nine Articles, Article XXV, 'Of the Sacraments'.

ordinance reserved, carried about, lifted up, or worshipped.[22]

The Cup of the Lord is not to be denied to the Lay-people; for both the parts of the Lord's Sacrament, by Christ's ordinance and commandment, ought to be ministered to all Christian men alike.[23]

They wanted to restore the original purity of Christ's sacraments, for they recognized that every addition only distracted from or distorted the gospel intention and clarity of those sacraments. They wanted to do what Christ had commanded, not more, and not less.

Here we see the wisdom of the Reformed policy of celebrating Christ's sacraments as he commanded without addition or subtraction. We see a clear example in Baptism. The practice of adding the giving of a candle to the ceremony of Baptism effects a profound theological change. The candle predominates as the powerful symbol, because when the water has been wiped away, the lighted candle remains. This changes the theological impact from washing to illumination, and from death and resurrection to the giving of celebratory light. This speaks of an easier and more Pelagian gospel, no doubt more acceptable in our society, but a reduction and distortion of the gospel truth.[24]

We now turn to the Holy Communion or Lord's Supper. This was the subject of deep controversy. We will focus on two issues: the presence of Christ, and the purpose of the service.

We consider the teaching of the Roman Catholic Council of Trent, which met in three sessions between 1545 and 1563. On the first issue, that of the presence of Christ, the teaching of Trent was that of Transubstantiation:

> And because that Christ, our Redeemer, declared that which He offered under the species of bread to be truly His own body, therefore has it ever been a firm belief in the Church of God, and this holy Synod doth now declare it anew, that, by

---

[22] Thirty-Nine Articles, Article XXVIII 'Of the Lord's Supper'.

[23] Thirty-Nine Articles, Article XXX, 'Of both kinds'.

[24] In my view requiring the use of the sign of the cross in Baptism contradicts the principle of not adding to the sacraments as they were instituted by Christ. But at least it points to the meaning of Baptism, Christ's death and resurrection.

the consecration of the bread and of the wine, a conversion is made of the whole substance of the bread into the substance of the body of Christ our Lord, and of the whole substance of the wine into the substance of His blood; which conversion is, by the holy Catholic Church, suitably and properly called Transubstantiation.[25]

This view was condemned in the *Thirty-Nine Articles*:

Transubstantiation (or the change of the substance of Bread and Wine) in the Supper of the Lord, cannot be proved by holy Writ; but is repugnant to the plain words of Scripture, overthroweth the nature of a Sacrament, and hath given occasion to many superstitions.[26]

And this was reinforced by the so-called 'Black Rubric' from the 1552 Book, omitted from Elizabeth's 1559 revision, and later reinserted at the end of the 1662 service of Holy Communion:

For the Sacramental Bread and Wine remain still in their very natural substances, and therefore may not be adored; (for that were Idolatry, to be abhorred of all faithful Christians;) and the natural Body and Blood of our Saviour Christ are in Heaven, and not here; it being against the truth of Christ's natural Body to be at one time in more places than one.

The second issue was of the purpose of the service. Trent taught that the Mass was propitiatory (it dealt with sin), and that it was a sacrifice, offered by the priests:

And forasmuch as, in this divine sacrifice which is celebrated in the mass, that same Christ is contained and immolated in an unbloody manner, who once offered Himself in a bloody manner on the altar of the cross; the holy Synod teaches, that this sacrifice is truly propitiatory...For the Lord, appeased by the oblation thereof, and granting the grace and gift of penitence, forgives even heinous crimes and sins. For the victim is one and the same, the same now offering by the

---

[25] The Decrees of the Council of Trent, http://history.hanover.edu/texts/trent.html, Decree concerning the most holy sacrament of the Eucharist, Chapter IV, 'On Transubstantiation'.
[26] Thirty-Nine Articles, Article XXVIII, 'Of the Lord's Supper'.

ministry of priests, who then offered Himself on the cross, the manner alone of offering being different.[27]

This doctrine too is condemned in the *Thirty-Nine Articles*:

> The Offering of Christ once made is that perfect redemption, propitiation, and satisfaction, for all the sins of the whole world, both original and actual; and there is none other satisfaction for sin, but that alone. Wherefore the sacrifices of Masses, in the which it was commonly said, that the Priest did offer Christ for the quick and the dead, to have remission of pain or guilt, were blasphemous fables, and dangerous deceits.[28]

And this Reformed view of the unique and completed sacrifice offered by Christ to the Father on the cross is reinforced by the language of the Holy Communion service itself in five ways:

i)   *Its focus on the complete efficacy and power of Christ's atonement, completed once for all in his death on the cross.*

We find this in the first Exhortation:

> ...we should alway remember the exceeding great love of our Master, and only Saviour, Jesus Christ, thus dying for us, and the innumerable benefits which by his precious blood-shedding he hath obtained to us...

We find it in the Comfortable Words:

> Hear what comfortable words our Saviour Christ saith unto all that truly turn to him. Come unto me all that travail and are heavy laden, and I will refresh you. St. Matth. xi. 28.

> So God loved the world, that he gave his only-begotten Son, to the end that all that believe in him should not perish, but have everlasting life. St. John iii. 16

> Hear also what St Paul saith:

---

[27]   Trent, Doctrine on the Sacrifice of the Mass, Chapter II, 'That the Sacrifice of the Mass is propitiatory both for the living and the dead'.

[28]   Thirty-Nine Articles, Article XXXI, 'Of the one Oblation of Christ finished upon the Cross'.

> This is a true saying, and worthy of all men to be received,
> That Christ Jesus came into the world to save sinners.
> 1 Tim i. 15

> If any man sin, we have an Advocate with the Father, Jesus
> Christ the righteous; and he is the propitiation for our sins.
> 1 St. John ii. 1.

And we find it in the prayer of consecration:

> Almighty God, our heavenly Father, who of thy tender mercy
> didst give thine only Son Jesus Christ to suffer death upon
> the Cross for our redemption; who made there (by his one
> oblation of himself once offered) a full, perfect, and sufficient
> sacrifice, oblation, and satisfaction, for the sins of the whole
> world...

ii)   *Its avoidance of any idea that the Holy Communion or Lord's
Supper is in itself a sacrifice.*

The word 'altar' is avoided, and it uses of the word 'sacrifice' carefully.
The Book of Common Prayer does not use the word 'altar': instead it
uses 'Table', 'Holy Table', 'Lord's Table'. It does not use the word
'altar' because that would imply a sacrifice. *The Book of Common
Prayer* does not use the word 'sacrifice' to refer to the conduct of the
service of Holy Communion. The word 'sacrifice' is used of the
response of praise after receiving communion, and of the offering of
our lives to God, but not of offering of bread and wine. Our sacrifice
is our response to God's mercy and God's feeding of us. The BCP
focuses on the complete efficacy and power of Christ's atonement,
completed once for all in his death on the cross. We find this in the
first Exhortation:

> O Lord and heavenly Father, we thy humble servants entirely
> desire thy fatherly goodness mercifully to accept this our
> sacrifice of praise and thanksgiving; most humbly beseeching
> thee to grant, that by the merits and death of thy Son Jesus
> Christ, and through faith in his blood, we and all thy whole
> Church may obtain remission of our sins, and all other
> benefits of his passion. And here we offer and present unto
> thee, O Lord, ourselves, our souls and bodies, to be a

reasonable, holy, and lively sacrifice unto thee...[29]

These Reformed truths are obscured today when the presence of Christ in the bread and wine is emphasized, when people call the Holy Table an 'altar', when there is emphasis on offering of bread and wine, and when the word 'Mass' is used to describe the service.

However we should not think that there is a return to the old idea of the Mass as a propitiatory sacrifice for sin. In much contemporary Anglicanism, the notion of sin has disappeared, as has the notion of atonement. So in much contemporary Anglicanism 'the sacrifice of Christ' and 'the sacrifice of the Eucharist' have nothing to do with sin and atonement. The idea is that Christ offered himself, and that self-offering is eternally continuing in heaven, and that we join in that offering in the Eucharist, as we offer ourselves with Christ. So in many contemporary liturgies, the atoning death of Christ once for all on the cross to deal with sin is strangely muted.[30]

And in general, services today tend to focus on our sacrifices to God, and these overshadow Christ's once for all sacrifice to God. *The Book of Common Prayer* rightly focuses on this work of God for our salvation.

iii)   *Catholic services focus on our offering to God, whereas the BCP focuses on our receiving of the sacrament.*

In the BCP the bread and wine are not brought forward as offerings, and they are received immediately after the Prayer of Consecration. The focus in the Bible is on our receiving in the Lord's Supper, not our offering. That is true in the gospel accounts of Christ's institution of this meal, as it is true in 1 Corinthians 10 and 11.[31]

iv)   *Catholic services of that time and today focus on the descent of Christ into the elements, whereas the BCP focuses on our raising*

---

[29]   BCP, Holy Communion.

[30]   See also A.M. Stibbs, *Sacrament, Sacrifice and Eucharist: the Meaning Function and Use of the Lord's Supper*, (London: The Tyndale Press, 1961); Martin Parsons, *The Holy Communion: An Exposition of the Prayer Book Service, The Prayer Book Commentaries*, (London: Hodder and Stoughton, 1961); and Griffith Thomas, *Principles*, pp. 414-426.

[31]   It is also true in John 6, for those who think that this chapter has sacramental relevance.

our eyes of faith to our glorious ascended Lord Christ in heaven, as we lift up our hearts in faith.

v)   Catholic services focus on the bread as the body of Christ, whereas the BCP focuses on the congregation as the body of Christ.

So there is less attention to respecting the elements of bread and wine, and more attention to respecting the church, the body of Christ.

2.2.3   *It ensures that other actions and ceremonies express Biblical truth*

Here the Church of England did not adopt the severe policy of limiting what was to be done in services to what was commanded in Scripture. Rigorously applied, that would not allow us to take weddings or funerals, collect money for the work of the local church, or give notices in our services! Likewise in daily life, it would not allow us to engage in education, the adoption of children, or the receiving of interest on our bank accounts, as there are no specific commands to do so in the Bible.[32]

The Church of England Reformers' policy comprised three principles: Biblical doctrine (meaning those doctrines taught and supported by the Bible) and edification (referring to growing people in Biblical faith), and the prohibition of actions that did not serve these priorities. We see these principles expressed in the following quotations:

> This our excessive multitude of Ceremonies was so great, and many of them so dark, that they did more confound and darken, than declare and set forth Christ's benefits unto us.[33]

> It is not necessary that Traditions and Ceremonies be in all places one, and utterly like; for at all times they have been divers, and may be changed according to the diversities of

---

[32]   D.G. Hart and John R. Mueller, *With Reverence and Awe: Returning to the Basics of Reformed Worship,* (Philippsburg: P&R, 2002), pp. 89-102, and pp. 145-158, defend a more conservative view, by distinguishing between elements and circumstances. But this does not solve the problem that we do not apply the strict regulative principle in our daily lives. See further, D.A. Carson, ed., *Worship by the Book,* (Grand Rapids: Zondervan, 2002), pp. 11-63.

[33]   BCP, 'Of Ceremonies'

countries, times, and men's manners, so that nothing be ordained against God's Word.[34]

The Romish Doctrine concerning Purgatory, Pardons, Worshipping, and Adoration as well of Images as of Reliques, and also invocation of Saints, is a fond thing vainly invented, and grounded upon no warranty of Scripture, but rather repugnant to the Word of God.[35]

Every particular or national Church hath authority to ordain, change, and abolish, ceremonies or rites of the Church ordained only by man's authority, so that all things be done to edifying.[36]

It is a thing plainly repugnant to the Word of God, and the custom of the Primitive Church, to have publick Prayer in the Church, or to minister the Sacraments in a tongue not understanded of the people.[37]

The implementation of this policy is seen very clearly in the Funeral service in *The Book of Common Prayer*. The focus of the service had changed radically from that of the Roman Catholic Church. In that service the focus was on praying for the person who had died, often including a Requiem Mass to remove punishment for the sin of the departed. This was roundly condemned in Article XXXI:

Wherefore the sacrifices of Masses, in the which it was commonly said, that the Priest did offer Christ for the quick and the dead, to have remission of pain or guilt, were blasphemous fables, and dangerous deceits.[38]

The service that replaced it has its focus on encouraging those present with the gospel certainty of the resurrection in Christ, and warning them to prepare for death and judgement. One of the sad

---

[34] Thirty-Nine Articles, Article XXXIV, 'Of the Traditions of the Church'.
[35] Thirty-Nine Articles, Article XXII, 'Of Purgatory'.
[36] Thirty-Nine Articles, Article XXXIV, 'Of the Traditions'.
[37] Thirty-Nine Articles, Article XXIV, 'Of speaking in the Congregation in such a tongue as the people understandeth'.
[38] Thirty-Nine Articles, Article XXXI, 'Of the one Oblation of Christ finished upon the Cross'.

features of Funerals today is how eulogies have tended to replace or overshadow sermons. The preaching of the word of God is lost.

So the policy was to ensure that all that was done in church was rigorously Biblical: that it conformed to and communicated Biblical doctrine, that where appropriate it followed Biblical commands, and that it served the edification of God's people.

The message of the BCP is that we approach God solely through Christ our great high priest and through his sacrificial blood, and that we may do so confident in God's mercy and his gospel promises.

When this is set aside, its replacements are manifestly inadequate and sinful. We may not approach God on the basis of our human qualities and contribution to the community. We do not gain access to God through the process of worship: worship is a response to our access to God through Christ's death, not its substitute. Music does not gain access to God, nor does the beauty of the building or décor: aesthetic appreciation is no replacement for the blood of Christ. The beauty of holiness in the New Testament is the beauty that is given us by our participation in Christ our substitute, and the moral beauty of lives transformed by his work in making us holy. Beauty in a building is a gift from God, but does not make it holy. God does not favour those who can afford beautiful buildings and paid choirs. And it is a common Charismatic, Catholic, and Romantic error to believe that music and worship is a means of access to God.[39] As the BCP reminds us, our access to God is solely through Christ our priest and his sacrifice on the cross:

> Therefore, my friends, since we have confidence to enter the sanctuary by the blood of Jesus, by the new and living way that he opened for us through the curtain (that is, through his flesh), and since we have a great priest over the house of God, let us approach with a true heart in full assurance of faith, with our hearts sprinkled clean from an evil conscience and our bodies washed with pure water. Let us hold fast to the confession of our hope without wavering, for he who has promised is faithful (Hebrews 10:19-23).

---

[39] This Anglican Foundations Series will in due course discuss the place of music in more detail – as indeed many other issues outlined in this booklet, which is intended as an overview of the riches we inherit in Anglican liturgy.

2.2.4 *It requires those in ministry to study the Bible, preach and teach the Bible, and to refute non-Biblical doctrines*

These themes are clearly expressed in three of the responses required of those to be made Bishops. The first is about what the person believes about the Bible, and whether the person will use the Bible and teach from it:

> Are you persuaded that the holy Scriptures contain sufficiently all doctrine required of necessity for eternal salvation through faith in Jesus Christ? And are you determined out of the same holy Scriptures to instruct the people committed to your charge, and to teach or maintain nothing as required of necessity to eternal salvation, but that which you shall be persuaded may be concluded and proved by the same?

The second requires the person to study and Bible and to ask God for help in understanding, and to use the Bible to teach sound doctrine and to stand against and convert those who oppose it:

> Will you then faithfully exercise yourself in the same holy Scriptures, and call upon God by prayer, for the true understanding of the same; so as ye may be able by them to teach and exhort with wholesome doctrine, and to withstand and convince the gainsayers?

The third requires the person to be diligent in refuting and driving away unbiblical doctrines, and to challenge others to do the same:

> Be you ready, with all faithful diligence, to banish and drive away all erroneous and strange doctrine contrary to God's Word; and both privately and openly to call upon and encourage others to the same?[40]

---

[40] The service then includes the presentation of a Bible to the candidate, to underline the fact that the person should study and teach the Bible: Then the Archbishop shall deliver him the Bible, saying,

> Give heed unto reading, exhortation, and doctrine. Think upon the things contained in this Book. Be diligent in them, that the increase coming thereby may be manifest unto all men. Take heed unto thyself, and to doctrine, and be diligent in doing them: for by so doing thou shalt both save thyself and them that hear thee.

And why is this necessary? The answer is found in part of one of the Bible readings set for the service of the consecration of a Bishop, words spoken by Paul to the elders at Ephesus:

> Take heed therefore unto yourselves, and to all the flock over the which the Holy Ghost hath made you overseers, to feed the Church of God, which he hath purchased with his own blood. For I know this, that after my departing shall grievous wolves enter in among you, not sparing the flock. Also of your own selves shall men arise speaking perverse things, to draw away disciples after them (Acts 20:28-30).[41]

So it was not enough for the 1662 Book itself to promote Biblical truth and preclude other ideas: those in ministry had to do the same in their preaching and teaching, and to encourage others in ministry to do the same. The 'very pure Word of God' must remain uncontaminated by merely human ideas which contradict, replace, confuse, or marginalise it.

2.3 In *The Book of Common Prayer* the Bible is to be read and to be preached, intentionally and systematically, and is the chief instrument of ministry

2.3.1 The Bible is to be read

Paul instructed Timothy: 'give attention to the public reading of Scripture', and, 'preach the word... with great patience and careful instruction' (1 Timothy 4:13, 2 Timothy 4:2).

It is possible to assert and preach Biblical truths, but to fail to read or preach the Bible in our services. *The Book of Common Prayer* was remarkable for its commitment to the reading of whole books of the Bible in the services of daily Morning and Evening Prayer. Those who attended church twice each day would hear most of the Old Testament once during a year and the New Testament twice a year:

> The Old Testament is appointed for the First Lessons at Morning and Evening Prayer, so as the most part thereof will be read every year once, as in the Calendar is appointed.

---

[41] All these quotations come from BCP, 'The Consecration of a Bishop or Archbishop'.

> The New Testament is appointed for the Second Lessons at Morning and Evening Prayer, and shall be read over orderly every year twice, once in the morning and once in the evening, besides the Epistles and Gospels, except the Apocalypse (the book of Revelation), out of which there are only certain Lessons appointed at the end of the year, and certain Proper Lessons appointed upon divers feasts.[42]

Previously the readings had been in Latin, which very few people understood, and these had been short readings taken from the Bible and elsewhere. Now the Bible was read in English, and was read so that people heard complete Bible books read sequentially, a continuous reading, or *lectio continua*. This reflected the mode of verbal revelation which God had used: not a series of short quotations out of context, but books of the Bible, each of which expressed a coherent message and pastoral purpose. This was a recovery of earlier practice which had been lost, as we read in the preface to the 1662 *Book of Common Prayer.*

> For they (in the Early Church) so ordered the matter, that all the whole Bible (or the greatest part thereof) should be read over once every year; intending thereby, that the Clergy, and especially such as were Ministers in the congregation, should (by often reading, and meditation in God's word) be stirred up to godliness themselves, and be more able to exhort others by wholesome doctrine, and to confute them that were adversaries to the truth; and further, that the people (by daily hearing of holy Scripture read in the Church) might continually profit more and more in the knowledge of God, and be the more inflamed with the love of his true Religion... But these many years passed, this godly and decent order of the ancient Fathers hath been so altered, broken, and neglected, by planting in uncertain Stories, and Legends, with multitude of Responds, Verses, vain Repetitions, Commemorations, and Synodals; that commonly when any Book of the Bible was begun, after three or four Chapters were read out, all the rest were unread... And for a readiness in this matter, here is drawn out a Calendar for that purpose,

---

[42] BCP, 'The Order how the rest of Holy Scripture is appointed to be read'.

which is plain and easy to be understood; wherein (so much as may be) the reading of holy Scripture is so set forth, that all things shall be done in order, without breaking one piece from another. For this cause be cut off Anthems, Responds, Invitatories, and such like things as did break the continual course of the reading of the Scripture.[43]

So here was another aspect of the Reformed commitment to 'the very pure Word of God'. Distractions from Scripture were to be set aside, along with unbiblical and anti-Biblical ideas.

The Medieval Church had asserted that the power of God was to be found in the sacraments: the Reformed church asserted the power of God in the Scriptures, including in reading them book by book in English. This focus on the use of vernacular language was a distinctive feature of the Reformation, as was evident in Luther's translation of the Bible into German, and the work of the French and Swiss Reformers.

We have to admit that the 1662 reading plan for the Bible on Sundays was less successful in terms of systematic reading of books of the Bible, because the readings for Sunday Morning and Evening Prayer mostly followed the daily lectionary, and the readings for Holy Communion were not organized to follow through books of the Bible.

A good lectionary is one that enables us to hear those distinct units of verbal revelation, the books of the Bible. A bad lectionary is one that ignores those units, and gives us a collection of readings out of their canonical contexts. These thematic excerpts depend on expert detailed knowledge of the Bible, and make no sense to people who are less learned than the devisers of the lectionary. Furthermore, they promote preaching on themes which do not do justice to any of the Bible texts that are used, and are often superficial in their use of Scripture. They remove the texts they use from their divine and human context, and do not model a good use of the Bible.

Those who abandon official lectionaries need to work very hard to ensure that they are not just selecting readings that reflect their own prejudices, and that the readings reflect the full richness of Scripture, including the Old Testament.

---

[43]   BCP, 'Concerning the Service'.

And as it is now common practice to have many different people reading the Bible in our services, it is essential that we chose people who are gifted in this ministry, that we train them in it, and that we explain to them that no-one is able to read the Bible publicly without preparation. I tell people who are to read the Bible aloud in church to practice every reading aloud and loudly at least three times! If people don't do this, you can hear the constant indecision in their voices about the meaning of the Bible passage and what they want to emphasize in their reading. Lay people who take any part in leading our services should be well-trained to do so, and all of us need to prepare our public reading of Scripture!

2.3.2   *The Bible is to be preached*

We find that the preaching and teaching of God's words is fundamental to ministry in the New Testament. Jesus Christ told his followers, 'Go therefore and make disciples of all nations', and Paul instructed Timothy, 'proclaim the message...convince, rebuke, and encourage, with the utmost patience in teaching' (Matthew 28:19, 2 Timothy 4:2). We read these words in Article XIX:

> The visible Church of Christ is a congregation of faithful men in the which the pure Word is preached and the sacraments be duly administered according to Christ ordinance.

The preaching of the pure Word of God was central principle of Reformed Anglicanism. By 'purity' they meant that the Word of God, the Bible, should not be mixed with impure substances, such as unbiblical traditions or ideas. The priority of this ministry was well expressed in the Bishop's exhortation in the Ordination of Priests:

> And now again we exhort you, in the Name of our Lord Jesus Christ, that you have in remembrance, into how high a dignity, and to how weighty an office and charge ye are called: that is to say, to be messengers, watchmen, and stewards of the Lord; to teach and to premonish, to feed and provide for the Lord's family; to seek for Christ's sheep that are dispersed abroad, and for his children who are in the midst of this naughty world, that they may be saved through Christ for ever.

The key Biblical images are that of messenger, watchmen and stewards. The messenger is one who proclaims a message from God, as did the prophets in the Old Testament and the disciples and apostles in the New Testament. A watchman, as in Ezekiel 16, is one who warns a city of a coming enemy. And a steward is one who administers the revealed mysteries of God in the saving work of Christ, as Paul wrote: 'Think of us in this way, as servants of Christ and stewards of God's mysteries' (1 Corinthians 4:1).

Preaching 'the very pure Word of God' to lay people was a novel idea. Monks had preached learned sermons in Latin in monasteries. Clergy had preached learned sermons in Latin in Cathedrals and at Court. Members of the Preaching Orders had preached popular wisdom and told the stories of saints in the fields and at Preaching Crosses. The preaching of the pure Word of God in English to lay people in local churches regularly Sunday by Sunday was a new idea, though the equivalent was common in the Early Church, as we see in the sermons of John Chrysostom and Augustine.[44] It was hard to find clergy who were ready for this ministry. To fill the gap, the *Book of Homilies* was produced so that those who would not preach could read a Homily instead. Heinrich Bullinger's *Decades* was another collection of authorized sermons. The published sermons of John Calvin were popular in England, and provided a model for preachers.[45] Able preachers were appointed as 'Lecturers' in churches, with the specific task of preaching sermons.[46] In some parishes, such as St Antholin's Budge Row in London, there were sermons each morning.[47] Some Puritans ran 'Prophesyings' which provided in-service training for clergy in expository preaching. Ministers would meet at a market-town, and hear three or four

---

[44] Expository Preaching of this kind died out because of the need for sermons that tackled issues of theological controversy, because there were fewer educated clergy, and because the liturgy increased in length and squeezed out the sermon! See Thomas K. Carroll, *Preaching the Word: The Message of the Fathers of the Church*, (Wilmington: Michael Glazier, 1984), pp. 63, 197, 206, 220.

[45] T.H.L. Parker, *Calvin's Preaching*, (Edinburgh: T&T Clark, 1992), pp. 72,73. Twenty-three editions and impressions of Calvin's sermons were published between 1550 and 1599.

[46] Paul S. Seaver, *The Puritan Lectureships*, (Stanford: Stanford University Press, 1970; and in Christopher Hill, *Society and Puritanism in Pre-Revolutionary England*, (London: Panther, 1969), see chapter 3, 'The Ratsbane (!) of Lecturing'.

[47] Lee Gatiss, 'The Grand Nursery of Puritanism: St. Antholin's as a Strategic Centre for Gospel Ministry', in Gatiss, ed., *Preachers, Pastors and Ambassadors*, pp. 3-48.

sermons on a passage of Scripture.[48] Some Puritan ministers began to train up future preachers as part of their regular ministry, running small 'nurseries for preachers' in their local churches. Puritan colleges were founded at the Universities to train people for Reformed ministry, such as Emmanuel College Cambridge. The Universities began to adopt the educational priorities of Humanism, which usefully focused on the teaching of Hebrew and Greek, and the study of the Old and New Testaments. Teaching and preaching the Bible to lay people eventually produced a new generation of preachers. Significant Puritan Anglican preachers included Richard Sibbes,[49] William Gouge, Thomas Adams, William Whitaker, and Thomas Mountford. And some Bishops modelled good preaching, notably Bishop John Jewel of Salisbury, and Archbishop Toby Matthews of York.[50]

George Herbert wrote of the dignity of preaching:

> The Countrey Parson preacheth constantly, the pulpit is his joy and his throne: ... The Parsons Method in handling of a text consists of two parts; first, a plain and evident declaration of the meaning of the text; and secondly, some choyce Observations drawn out of the whole text, as it lyes entire, and unbroken in the Scripture it self. [51]

And Christopher Wren, architect of St Paul's Cathedral London and many city churches after the great fire of London in 1665, wrote of the purpose of church buildings:

> The Romanists, indeed, may build larger churches, it is enough if they hear the murmur of the Mass, and see the Elevation of the Host, but ours are to be fitted for Auditories...To hear the service, and both to hear distinctly,

---

[48]   Collinson, *Grindal,* pp. 233-242.
[49]   Mark Dever, *Richard Sibbes: Puritanism and Calvinism in Late Elizabethan and Early Stuart England,* (Macon: Mercer University Press, 2000).
[50]   For an outline of English Reformation preaching, see Philip Edgcumbe Hughes, 'Preaching, Homilies, and Prophesyings in Sixteenth Century England', *Churchman,* 89/1, 1975, pp. 7-32.
[51]   George Herbert, The Priest to the Temple, or, The Country Parson, chapter VII, in F.E. Hutchinson, ed., *The Works of George Herbert,* (Oxford: Clarendon Press, 1941), pp. 232-235.

and see, the Preacher.[52]

John Donne, better known as a poet, regarded preaching as the heart of his ministry as Dean of St Paul's Cathedral London. Donne was a good example of a pre-Laudian and pre-Caroline Reformation Anglican of the Jacobean Church.[53] David Edwards wrote of Donne: 'He belonged to the sizeable group in the Church under James I which in important ways Puritan without being fully Calvinist'.[54] For Donne, preaching was the heart of ministry: 'It hath been my desire (and God may be pleased to grant it to me) that I might die in the pulpit'.[55]

Donne's concern was for Gospel truth, proclamation, and fruitfulness, the conversion of many to Jesus Christ. No wonder his constant cry was *Væ mihi si non euangelizavero,* 'Woe to me if I do not preach the Gospel'.[56] If the Bible is the word of God about his Son and his Gospel, then how is this message to be communicated? 'By Preaching'. Preaching is a miracle, the direct work of God. 'But to doe great works by small means, to bring men to heaven by Preaching in the Church, this is a miracle'.[57] For preaching is the means by which we learn of Christ:

'Preaching must be a continuall application of all that Christ Jesus said and did, and suffered, to thee'.[58]

How then does God value preaching?

---

[52] As quoted in Horton Davies, *Worship and Theology in England,* Volume 1, (Grand Rapids: Eerdmans, 1966), p. 44.

[53] William Laud, Bishop of London 1628, then Canterbury 1633, promoted and enforced anti-Puritan policies, Arminian theology, and pre-Reformation liturgy. Charles I became King in 1625, and the Caroline Divines were High Church leaders (including Laud), whose ideas and policies he promoted

[54] David L. Edwards, *John Donne, Man of Flesh and Spirit,* (London/New York: Continuum, 2001), p. 319.

[55] William R. Mueller, *John Donne: Preacher,* (Princeton: Princeton University Press, 1962), p. 3.

[56] E.g. John Donne , *The Sermons of John Donne,* Volumes I – Io, eds., M.R. Potter, and E.M. Simpson, (Berkeley: University of California Press, 1953-1962), Vols. II, pp. 164, 308, IV, pp. 192, 195, 374, VI, p. 93, IX, p. 285, X, p. 126. This quotation from 1 Corinthians 9:16 had also been the motto of Bishop John Jewel.

[57] Donne, *Sermons,* VII, pp. 300, 301

[58] Donne, *Sermons,* VII, p. 232

There is no salvation but by faith, nor faith but by hearing, nor hearing but by preaching; and they that thinke meanliest of the Keyes of the Church, and speak faintliest of the Absolution of the Church, will yet allow, That those Keyes lock, and unlock in Preaching, That Absolution is conferred, or withheld in Preaching, That the proposing of the promises of the Gospel in Preaching, is that binding and loosing on earth, which bindes and looses in heaven.[59]

So the ministry of preaching has priority over sacraments:

For Sacraments were instituted by Christ, as subsidiary things, in a greater part, for our infirmity, who stand in need of such visible and sensible assistances. Christ preached the Christian Doctrine, long before he instituted the Sacraments.[60]

Donne had a high view of the work of God in the sacraments instituted by Christ,[61] but an even higher view of preaching:

As there lies always upon God's Minister a *væ si non*, Wo be unto me, if I preach not the Gospel, if I apply not the comfortable promises of the Gospel, to all that grone under the burden of their sins.[62]

God addresses his people now the words of ancient texts:

'God continues his speech, and speaks to us every day; still we must hear *Evangelium in sermone*, the Gospel in the Word'.[63]

He pointed to Christ's command:

Go ye, and preach: Because I (Christ) have all power, for preaching, take yee part of my power, and preach too...Preaching then being God's Ordinance, to beget Faith, to take away preaching, were to disarme God, and to quench the spirit.[64]

---

[59] Donne, *Sermons*, VII, p. 320.
[60] Donne, *Sermons*, X, p. 69.
[61] Donne, *Sermons*, VII, p. 321.
[62] Donne, *Sermons*, II, p. 164.
[63] Donne, *Sermons*, I, p. 291.
[64] Donne, *Sermons*, IV, p. 195.

So to lose preaching is to risk losing Christ:

> (S)o how long soever Christ have dwelt in any State, or any Church, if he grows speechless, he is departing: if there be a discontinuing, or slackening of preaching, there is a danger of losing Christ.[65]

Unfortunately, the practice of preaching in the Church of England did not live up to the rhetoric. There were two reasons for this. Firstly, while the Lectionary for daily Morning and Evening Prayer followed through books of the Bible, the Sunday Morning and Evening Prayer readings did not do this, and neither did the readings for Holy Communion. So, those who preached from the set readings would not expound a book of the Bible sequentially Sunday by Sunday.

Secondly, although Calvin's model of expository preaching was followed by some, other less helpful models of preaching predominated. The Homilies contained doctrine and ethics, but did not attempt to expound the Scriptures book by book. They were provided for use when clergy were largely ignorant of the Gospel, and not equipped to expound the Scriptures, and when there was a strong desire to control what was preached. They were necessary at the time, but not a good long-term model. And the predominant method of preaching adopted by Anglican Puritans was not Calvin's expository style, which aimed to project the sequential eloquence of a book of the Bible. They reverted to the more complicated Medieval model, in which a short text was analysed in great detail, followed with many points under Doctrine, and then Use (or application). So preaching tended to be Doctrinal, or applicatory, focused on small units of Bible text, but not sequentially expositional of the whole text of books of Scripture. And the general pattern of Anglican preaching came to be a mild example of the Medieval and Puritan model, with a short 'text' followed by general comments of application. It was no doubt the need to adhere rigidly to every aspect of the 1662 Book, including the Sunday Lectionary, that made it difficult to expound books of the Bible in Sunday sermons.

---

[65] Donne, *Sermons*, VII, p. 157. See further on Donne's preaching, Peter Adam, 'To bring men to heaven by preaching: John Donne's Evangelistic Sermons', reprinted in Gatiss, *Preachers, Pastors and Ambassadors*, pp. 261-292.

Those who followed Calvin's model of expository preaching included Bishops John Jewel and James Pilkington, both of whom had been Marian exiles in Geneva, and so would have seen Calvin's preaching first-hand.[66] Clergy included William Goudge, who preached on Hebrews for thirty years on Wednesday nights at St Ann's Blackfriars,[67] and Thomas Adams.[68] Archbishop Robert Leighton of Glasgow was also a great expositor.[69] In the general failure to adopt Biblical expository preaching, a great opportunity was lost, and it was not widely recovered until the 20th Century by the ministries and examples of John Stott and Dick Lucas.

It is not that expository preaching is the only valid form of preaching. We need to preach topical sermons, not least so we show people how to begin with a contemporary issue and find out God's wisdom and teaching in the Bible. And an expository style can fall into the trap of just 'teaching the Bible' without making use of it to 'convince, rebuke, and encourage' (2 Timothy 4:2), for the Bible should be a means, not an end in itself. It can fall into other traps too: mere moralism, mere devotionalism, or going so slowly through books of the Bible that it loses the flow of the book, and each verse becomes an opportunity to cover the whole Bible! We need expository preaching that respects and expounds books of the Bible, that is theological, devotional, and practical, and that teaches people how to read the Bible for themselves.

May God rid us of preaching that does not attempt to use the Bible at all, or that uses it superficially, or that uses the Bible text as a launching-pad to other ideas which then shape the content of the sermon.

---

[66] John Jewel, 'An Exposition upon the two Epistles of the Apostle St Paul to the Thessalonians', in *Writings of John Jewel*, (London: Religious Tract Society, nd), pp. 83-288, and James Pilkington, 'Exposition upon the Prophet Haggai, Exposition upon the Prophet Obadiah, Exposition upon certain chapter in Nehemiah', in *The Works of James Pilkington*, The Parker Society, (Cambridge: The University Press, 1842), pp. 1-496.

[67] See William Goudge, *Commentary on Hebrews*, (Grand Rapids: Kregel, 1980).

[68] Thomas Adams, *An Exposition of 2 Peter*, (Birmingham: Solid Ground Christian Books, 2008).

[69] Robert Leighton, 'A Practical Commentary on the First Epistle General of St Peter', *The Whole Works of Robert Leighton*, Vol. I, (ed.), J.N. Pearson, (London: James Duncan, 1835), pp. 109-609.

2.3.3   *The Bible is to be read and taught to lay people*

Here was another dramatic change brought about by the Reformation. The Roman Catholic Church had worked on the principle that the Bible was for clergy and monks, and not for lay people. That was why it was read in Latin in church, though very few lay people could understand that language. As lay people could not understand the Bible, the means of edification used for them was images, statues, and windows. As Pope Gregory had decided, 'images are the books of the uneducated'.[70] The usual sermons heard by lay people in the Medieval Church were either in Latin, or were the popular sermons given by visiting monks at open air Preaching Crosses. These were in English, but they were not based on the Bible, and did not intend to teach or explain the Bible. There would be references to the Bible, but mixed up with stories of the saints and popular wisdom and teaching of the church.[71] They did not train lay people to understand the Bible or read it for themselves: anyway the only Bibles available were in Latin, and were too expensive to own, and most lay people were illiterate. So when Richard Greenham was appointed to Dry Drayton outside Cambridge in 1570 as the first Reformation minister, he discovered that the people knew nothing of the Bible, and the churchwardens were unable to write their names.[72]

Here are radical words from Cranmer's Preface to the second edition of the *Great Bible*, the first authorized translation into English, placed in churches in 1540:

> For the Holy Ghost hath so ordered and attempered (tuned) the Scriptures, that in them as well publicans, fishers and shepherds may find their edification, as well as great doctors (scholars) their erudition (learning)... In the Scriptures be the fat pastures of the soul; therein is no venomous meat, no unwholesome thing; there be the very dainty and pure feeding. He that is ignorant will find there what he should

---

[70] As quoted in John Calvin, *Institutes of the Christian Religion,* vol. 1, tr. Ford Lewis Battles, The Library of Christian Classics, Vol. XX, (Philadelphia: Westminster Press, 1960), I.XI.5, p. 105.

[71] Hugh Latimer preached a Reformed version of this popular style.

[72] John H. Primus, *Richard Greenham: the portrait of an Elizabethan pastor,* (Macon: Mercer University Press, 1998), pp. 24-32.

learn. He that is a perverse sinner shall there find his damnation to make him fear and tremble. He that laboureth to serve God shall find there his glory, and the promissions (promises) of eternal life, exhorting him more diligently to labour...[73]

There are similar claims in the Homily, 'The Reading of Holy Scripture':

Unto a Christian man there can be nothing either more necessary or profitable than the knowledge of holy Scripture: forasmuch as in it is contained God's true Word, setting forth his glory and also man's duty. And there is no truth nor doctrine necessary for our justification and everlasting salvation, but that is or may be drawn out of that fountain and well of truth.[74]

But is the Scripture too dangerous to read?

Read it humbly, with a meek and a lowly heart, to the intent that you may glorify God, and not yourself, with the knowledge of it; and do not read it without daily praying to God that he would direct your reading to good effect.[75]

Or is it too difficult to read?

God receiveth the learned and the unlearned, and casteth away none...And the Scripture is full, as well of low valleys, plain ways, and easy for every one to use, as also of high hills and mountains, which few men can climb unto.[76]

This change of theology was reflected in the removal of images, paintings, and windows, and their replacement by the words of the Bible painted or inscribed on the walls of churches, so that church interiors became 'a giant scrapbook of Scripture'.[77] These included the Ten Commandments and The Lord's Prayer, as well as the Apostles' Creed.

---

[73] Preface to the Great Bible, in Bray, *Documents,* pp. 237,238.
[74] Homily, 'Holy Scripture', (part one), p. 1.
[75] Homily, 'Holy Scripture', (part two), p. 7.
[76] Homily, 'Holy Scripture', (part two), p. 7.
[77] MacCulloch, *The Boy King,* p. 159.

As Hilary Mantel has written of the early stages of the Reformation:

> They have seen their religion painted on the walls of churches, or carved in stone, but now God's pen is poised, and he is ready to write his words in the books of their hearts.[78]

For, as John Donne preached, 'The Scriptures are God's Voyce; The Church is his Eccho.'[79] And, as Jesus Christ taught us:

> It is written, "One does not live by bread alone, but by every word that comes from the mouth of God" (Matthew 4:4).

The teaching of the Bible to lay people had a big impact on England, not least in enabling them to gain confidence in knowing God through the Scriptures. It also raised the standard of clergy, for they now came to training already Biblically literate, and so more ready to learn more deeply in their preparation for ministry.

2.3.4   *The Bible is the chief instrument of ministry*

A major issue at the Reformation was that of how God worked within Christian people to change them. The Roman Catholic Church had taught that the Sacraments were the main means of transforming grace. The Reformers asserted that the Word of God was the main means of grace, following the words of Jesus Christ to his disciples, 'You have already been cleansed by the word that I have spoken to you' (John 15:2).

So we read in Cranmer's Preface to the Great Bible:

> (A)s mallets, hammers, saws, chisels...be the tools of their occupation, so be the books of the prophets and apostles, and all Holy Writ inspired by the Holy Ghost, the instruments of our salvation.

In the Medieval ordination services, those ordained were handed a Patten (Communion plate) or Chalice (Communion cup), symbols of the Mass, as a reminder of the central act of their ministry.

---

[78]   Hilary Mantel, *Wolf Hall*, (London: Fourth Estate, 2009), p. 516.
[79]   Donne, *Sermons*, VI, p. 223.

Archbishop Cranmer made the first change in the 1550 Ordinal, attached to the 1549 Prayer Book, where we read:

> The Bishop shall deliver to every one of them, the Bible in the one hand, and the Chalice or cup with the bread in the other, and saying...

So the message was that their ministries were to be achieved by the Bible as well as by the sacrament. The second change was made in the 1552 Ordinal, where we read:

> The Bishop shall deliver to every one of them the Bible in his hand, saying...

So now the central means of ministry was to be the Bible. This same doctrine and practice was retained in the 1662 *Book of Common Prayer*, and demonstrated the Reformed theology of ordained ministry of the Church of England. Similarly, in the service for the Consecration of Bishops, the Bishop was to be handed a Bible, as a reminder of the central role of the Bible in Episcopal ministry.

This confidence in the power of the Bible as the chief means of ministry is based on its own God-given power, as expressed in the words of the homily, 'The Reading of Holy Scripture'. For this Homily expressed great confidence in the power of the Bible to convert and to change people. They not only believed in the authority of the Bible: they also believed in its power:

> The words of Holy Scripture be called the words of everlasting life; for they be God's instrument, ordained for the same purpose. They have power to turn through God's promise, and they be effectual through God's assistance; and, being received in a faithful heart, they have ever an heavenly spiritual working in them... And there is nothing that so much strengtheneth our faith and trust in God, that so much keepeth up innocence and pureness of the heart and also of outward godly life and conversation, as continual reading and recording of God's word. For that thing which, by continual use of reading of holy Scripture, and diligent searching of the same, is deeply printed and graven in the heart, at length turneth almost into nature...there is nothing that more maintaineth godliness of the mind, and drives away ungodliness, than doth the continual reading or hearing of God's word, if it be joined with a godly mind and a good

affection to know and follow God's will... For the Scripture of God is the heavenly meat of our souls: the hearing and keeping of it maketh us blessed, sanctifieth us, and makes us holy: it turneth our souls; it is a light lantern to our feet: it is a sure, steadfast and everlasting instrument of salvation: it gives wisdom to the humble and lowly-hearted: it comforteth, maketh glad, cheereth, and cherishes our consciences...[80]

The Bible is God-given as the main means of ministry. It is used by God to convert to faith in Christ, to bring assurance of salvation, to transform character, to create mature churches, and transform nations. The Bible produces effective culture-change. This is why the BCP wants to preserve and communicate 'the very pure Word of God'.

Here are some reasonable questions to all who have received a New Testament or Bible at their ordination.

Are you still studying the Bible? How long is it since you have learnt something new from the Bible, or changed the way you live in response to the Bible? Are you shaping your life of faith and obedience by the Bible?

Do you use the Bible and teach the content of Bible in your sermons and homilies? Do you project the message of the Bible passage in your sermons? Do you have a long-term plan of Bible teaching in your preaching? Do you use the Bible and teach from the Bible in your public and private evangelism? Do you use the Bible in training people for ministry? Do you use the Bible in your counselling and mentoring? Are you equipping people to read and understand the Bible for themselves?

When you preach, have you fallen into the habit of not using or quoting from the Bible? When you preach do you tend to use the Bible text as a launching-pad for other ideas, and then preach those other ideas? Do you fall into the trap of assuming Biblical knowledge, literacy and background which may not exist? Are you aware of your ten favourite ideas which are likely to provide the application in your sermons, whatever your text? Do you preach 'the very pure Word of

---

[80]   The Homily, 'The Reading of Holy Scripture', (part one), p. 3. Quotations from Scripture are highlighted in the Homily.

God'? We should remember the advice of St Augustine, 'For to believe what you please, and not to believe what you please, is to believe yourselves, and not the gospel'[81].

2.4 *The Book of Common Prayer provides responses to God that express Bible truths and use Bible words.*

Moses instructed the people of God that God's words must be in their hearts and on their lips:

> Keep these words that I am commanding you today in your heart. Recite them to your children and talk about them when you are at home and when you are away, when you lie down and when you rise (Deuteronomy 6:6,7).

One remarkable feature of the Bible is that it contains not only the direct words of God mediated through human agents, but also words of response to that revelation. So for example, although the Book of Psalms includes many quotations of the verbal revelation of God, it is essentially a wide collection of human responses to God. These human responses are part of the inspired Scriptures, but their form is that of response to God in prayer, praise, lament, confession, intercession, complaint, resolve and promise. The intention of the book of Psalms was that his people said or sang the Psalms. So the Bible comes not only in the form of instruction, but also gives God's people verbal responses to that instruction. The people of God are to repeat the words that God has spoken to them, and to repeat the words he has given them to respond to him. Biblical revelation occurred both in what God said, and also in what he told his people to say. So the Bible shapes our verbal response to God, as it shapes our whole response to God, by including spoken, written, and lived examples of that response. Similarly, we base our response to God on his words to us. John Calvin wrote:

> There is nothing more efficacious in our prayers than to set his own word before God, and then to found our

---

[81] Augustine, *Contra Faustum*, Book XVII, 3. http://www.newadvent.org/fathers/140617.htm

supplications upon his promises, as if he dictated to us out of his own mouth what we are to ask.[82]

This is exactly what we find in the great prayers of the Bible. So, for example, the long prayer found in Nehemiah 9:6-37 is a patchwork of Bible verses.[83] Similarly, when Hannah, Mary, Zechariah, and Simeon praised God they used both references to and words from their Bibles.[84] We pray, praise, lament and promise best when we use words that God himself has given us, because they reveal God to us, and show us how he wants us to respond. God's words are to be in our hearts and on our lips.

Charles Simeon, in his sermons on 'The Excellency of the Liturgy' (that is, *The Book of Common Prayer*) challenged his hearers to record spontaneous prayers prayed in churches over a year, and compare their Biblical content with the prayers of the 1662 Prayer Book![85] He expected that the BCP prayers would have more Biblical content. In fact, people who know their Bibles well often include Bible truths and words in their prayers: but many do not.

And we equip lay people for effective mutual ministry and evangelism by training them to speak the very words of God.

It is not just that the prayers of *The Book of Common Prayer* express Bible truths in Bible words. Passages of Scripture are also used extensively to respond to God. So the daily recitation of the Psalms, by which all the Psalms are read by the congregation each month in Morning and Evening Prayer is a major way in which the Bible is used in response to God. Of special focus here is Psalm 95, recited daily in Morning Prayer, with its solemn warning so appropriate in the context of the public reading of the Bible: 'Today if ye will hear his voice, harden not your hearts' (Psalm 95:7,8, BCP).

So also the Versicles and Responses and most of the Canticles are also from the Bible. The Morning and Evening Prayer Canticles

---

[82]   John Calvin, *Commentary on the Four Books of Moses*, Calvin Translation Society, Vol. IV. (Reprinted, Grand Rapids: Baker, 1981), p 75.

[83]   See Jacob M. Myers, *Ezra, Nehemiah*, The Anchor Bible, (New York: Doubleday, 1965), pp. 167-169

[84]   1 Samuel 2: 1-10, Luke 1: 46-55, 67-79, and 2:29-32.

[85]   See Andrew Atherstone, *Charles Simeon on "The Excellency of the Liturgy"*, (Norwich: Canterbury Press, 2012).

included Psalms 67, 95, 98 and 100; Luke 1:46-55, 68-79, and Luke 2:29-32. The famous 'Easter Anthem' is a skilful collection of verses from Romans and 1 Corinthians:

> Christ our passover is sacrificed for us: therefore let us keep the feast; Not with the old leaven, nor with the leaven of malice and wickedness: but with the unleavened bread of sincerity and truth. 1 Corinthians 5:7.

> Christ being raised from the dead dieth no more: death hath no more dominion over him. For in that he died, he died unto sin once: but in that he liveth, he liveth unto God. Likewise reckon ye also yourselves to be dead indeed unto sin: but alive unto God, through Jesus Christ our Lord. Romans 6:9.

> Christ is risen from the dead: and become the first-fruits of them that slept. For since by man came death: by man came also the resurrection of the dead. For as in Adam all die: even so in Christ shall all be made alive. 1 Corinthians 15:20.

> Glory be to the Father, and to the Son: and to the Holy Ghost; As it was in the beginning, is now, and ever shall be: world without end. Amen.

And the Canticles that are not taken from the Bible, such as the *Te Deum*, also include Biblical truths and words, and as do the Creeds.[86]

So the people of God are taught and edified not only by the reading and preaching of Scripture, but also by the Bible-shaped response they made in the words they said in the services. It is the book of 'Common Prayer', not least in that prepared prayers enable the congregation to say the prayers together, whereas spontaneous prayers preclude this practice.

What honours God edifies people, and edification is a strategic aim of the 1662 Book. Some ceremonies were discarded because they obscured God's glory, and edification was the purpose:

> Of such Ceremonies as be used in the Church, and have had their beginning by the institution of man, some at the first were of godly intent and purpose devised, and yet at length

---

[86] See John R.W. Stott, *Canticles and Selected Psalms, The Prayer Book Commentaries*, (London: Hodder and Stoughton, 1966).

turned to vanity and superstition: some entered into the Church by undiscreet devotion, and such a zeal as was without knowledge; and for because they were winked at in the beginning, they grew daily to more and more abuses, which not only for their unprofitableness, but also because they have much blinded the people, and obscured the glory of God, are worthy to be cut away, and clean rejected: other there be, which although they have been devised by man, yet it is thought good to reserve them still, as well for a decent order in the Church, (for the which they were first devised) as because they pertain to edification, whereunto all things done in the Church (as the Apostle teacheth) ought to be referred.[87]

The same focus on edification is repeated in the same preface:

This our excessive multitude of Ceremonies was so great, and many of them so dark, that they did more confound and darken, than declare and set forth Christ's benefits unto us. And besides this, Christ's Gospel is not a Ceremonial Law, (as much of Moses' Law was,) but it is a Religion to serve God, not in bondage of the figure or shadow, but in the freedom of the Spirit; being content only with those Ceremonies which do Serve to a decent Order and godly Discipline, and such as be apt to stir up the dull mind of man to the remembrance of his duty to God, by some notable and special signification, whereby he might be edified.[88]

One church I visited recently had an excellent service, as well as an excellent sermon. Unlike many churches which have dispensed with a prayer book, this service had a gospel shape, the Bible reading was of high standard, there was a creative confession and statement of forgiveness, the intercessions extended beyond the needs of the congregation, and embraced the church and the world, and the songs were Biblical! I made enquiry of how this miracle had happened! The answer was that they have carefully prepared six services, with all the right ingredients, and use them in rotation. Each of those is carefully planned, and there is good variety among the six services, but also

---

[87] BCP, 'Of Ceremonies'.
[88] BCP, 'Of Ceremonies'.

continuity and gospel purpose. All the services were intentionally Biblical, as, of course, were the sermons.

This was unusual, because, as we easily get into a reductive rut in our daily personal prayers, so churches easily get into a reductive rut. And as we easily reinforce unhelpful ideas in our personal prayers, so extemporary or unprepared prayers, or poorly chosen songs in church services can do the same. Likewise, people who lead intercessions without instruction often fail to pray for the world and the church, as we are clearly instructed to do in 1 Timothy 2: 1-7. Their prayers are often limited to the local church, and to the personal needs of those in trouble.

When I hear someone pray, 'we just ask that you would bless them...' I think to myself that the Bible gives us theological substance for our intercessions, and good models of how to pray deep, rich, and passionate prayers. When I am leading intercessions, I find it very useful to prepare using the Bible, so that my prayers are enriched and deepened by the Bible. I try to include quotations from the Bible, and Bible words, so that people make the connections between what we are praying and what the Bible teaches us about God, his gospel, world, and church.[89] We want to show people the value of turning the Bible into prayers. As I expect people to prepare their leading of a service, and the intercessions, so I also want them to ensure that the songs and hymns we sing reflect Biblical truth.

Furthermore, it is a great pity when songs and hymns do not reflect a healthy variety. We should have some in each service that are theologically dense; and some that feature just one theological theme in each verse, or one for the whole song. We should have some that use the language of individuals ('I', 'me'); and others that use the language of community ('We', 'us'). We should have some that are rich in Biblical language; and others that use plainer words, more commonly understood in our society. We should have some that are focused on God, who God is, and what God has done; and others that

---

[89] As indeed in my own prayers, I often find it helpful to prepare set prayers, which I pray every day. Here is a short example: 'Dear heavenly Father, please make me the person you want me to be, prepare me to do the good works you want me to do, and help me to do them'. This prayer is based on Ephesians 2:9-10.

are focused on our response to God. And we need to ensure that our songs cover a good range of central Biblical and theological themes.

In terms of musical style, we have difficult choices to make, because we do not live in societies with one universal musical style and taste. There are many musical sub-cultures, and while the music I like attracts me, and music I don't like repels me! Unfortunately, to favour some is to discriminate against others. There are two useful guidelines. The first is to try to train the congregation to cope with, if not enjoy, a variety of musical tastes. For the narrower the musical tolerance of a congregation, the narrower the group of people who will join. The second is to use musical styles that both express the congregation who are present, and also would be acceptable to those we want to attract. It is also possible to develop congregations on the basis of the homogenous musical taste unit church growth principle: these have the advantages and disadvantages of the homogenous unit church growth principle!

One clear instruction in the Scripture about what we do when we meet is that we should speak and sing, and that purposes of the speaking and singing are that we should encourage, admonish and edify each other, and also sing and speak to the Lord, giving thanks to God the Father (1 Corinthians 14:3,12,26, Ephesians 4:12,29, 5:19,20, Colossians 3:16,17). The BCP makes room for this, with the congregation saying and singing the responses, the psalms, the canticles, the creeds, and some prayers. And when we add hymns and songs, there is even more scope for this congregational participation.

There are two current musical traditions that inhibit this ministry of the congregation. The first is the style of cathedrals and college chapels, in which a professional choir sings most if not all of these parts of the service on behalf of and instead of the congregation. I enjoy the music, but grieve at the exclusion, and at the frustration of the intention of *The Book of Common Prayer*.

The second style is common in more informal services, when a Band 'leads the worship', equipped with loud-speakers and drums. This music is often so loud, that it is impossible to hear the voices of people around us singing, and so we are not able to encourage, admonish and edify each other or to receive this ministry. We need to put some pillows in the drums, and turn down the amplifier, otherwise the musicians and singers so dominate the singing, that even though the singing is meant to be a mutual ministry of the congregation, we are rendered inaudible by the decibels of the Band! They are using a performance style which does not serve the mutual ministry of congregational singing.

Moreover, performance style modern songs are not always designed to be sung by congregations. Songs for congregations need have limited variation in pitch, speed, and predictability, or they are self-defeating, because they are not able to be sung by untrained people. And, of course their theology needs constant attention. When theologically untrained musicians dominate the service we are in trouble. Music is a good servant but a bad master, in both formal and informal settings! The Reformers worked hard at producing congregation-friendly models of singing.[90] We need to do the same for our time.

We should also learn from the Collects of *The Book of Common Prayer.* The idea of a Collect is that it is a short prayer that summarises one aspect of our response to God. We could use a prepared Collect effectively after each Bible reading, or at the end of a sermon. I often write a Collect for a sermon, pray it at the start of the sermon, and then get everyone to pray it at the end of the sermon. The BCP Collects provide great models of such prayers. They begin with who God is and or what God has done. They then make a request in response this God. They then give the purpose of our asking. They conclude with the basis of our asking, through Christ.[91]

Take for example the Collect for the second Sunday in Advent:

> Blessed Lord, who caused all holy Scriptures to be written for our learning: Grant that we may in such wise hear them, read, mark, learn, and inwardly digest them, that by patience and comfort of thy holy Word, we may embrace and ever hold fast the blessed hope of eternal life, which thou hast given us in our Saviour Jesus Christ. Amen.

---

[90] R.A. Leaver, *The Work of John Marbeck,* (Oxford: Sutton Courtenay Press, 1978).

[91] For an excellent study of the BCP Collects, see L.E.H. Stephens-Hodge, *The Collects: An Introduction and Exposition, The Prayer Book Commentaries,* (London: Hodder and Stoughton, 1966).

And they are informed by Scripture. So this Collect includes references to 2 Timothy 3:16,17; Ezekiel 3:1-3; and Romans 15:4. Similarly the Collect for St Simon and St Jude is a wonderful prayer based on Ephesians 2:19-22.

> O Almighty God, who has built thy Church upon the foundation of the Apostles and Prophets, Jesus Christ himself being the head corner-stone: Grant us so to be joined together in unity of spirit by their doctrine, that we may be made an holy temple acceptable unto thee; through Jesus Christ our Lord. Amen.[92]

Of course the language used for the services is English, not Latin. Here is a good Biblical and Reformation principle at work, that of using the language of the people. It is wonderful that we have a translatable Bible, and that it is as powerful in translation as it is in its original languages. But notice that there is no 'dumbing-down' in the BCP in the language of the Bible or of the services. It is not the simplest language possible, it does not avoid Bible words, and it does not avoid deep theology. Biblical and theological words are used, and the people are expected to grow and learn what they mean, as of course they will, if they are taught the Scriptures. We should use the full variety of Bible language in our spoken and sung response to God. We will find that the casual, relaxed informal language style of close friends will not be adequate to convey the full variety of Biblical eloquence. Nor will formal and restrained language be adequate for the task. We need to match the full range of Biblical language in our response to God.

This is important for three reasons. The first is that the Bible is not a contemporary document, but a message from the past. As we look back in time to God's saving work in Christ Jesus, so we have to learn to look back in time to the verbal revelation of God in the Bible. The second is that people need to learn Biblical and theological language if they are to read the Bible: if we avoid such language in church, they will be ill-equipped to read the Bible on their own. The third is that while a reduced-language gospel may bring people to conversion, only the full verbal revelation of God will bring them to maturity. The language of the 1662 Book was the language of the

---

[92]   I would have written 'Spirit' to make it clear that the Holy Spirit is intended.

people, but it was also Biblical language. And the language of *The Book of Common Prayer*, like the language of the 1611 Authorised Version of the Bible, was appropriately the language of public declaration of the people of God, not the private and informal language of close friends. May all the fullness of 'the very pure Word of God' be found on our lips and in our lives.

3   Summary

We see that the 1662 *Book of Common Prayer* is comprehensively Biblical, and its Biblical identity comprises four dynamics:

- *It is intentionally formed by Biblical truth, and focused on the gospel of Christ.*

  This provides overall theological coherence. Without it, there would be a danger of believing that the mere use of Bible words would ensure Bible truths, or the danger of finding substitute revelation and another gospel.

- *It precludes and corrects un-Biblical and anti-Biblical doctrines and practices.*

  This brings theological and intellectual clarity, and helps to repudiate ideas that undermine the fundamental identity of Christianity. Without it, the church would drift from the truth, or be captured by error.

- *The Bible is to be both read and preached, intentionally and systematically, and is the chief instrument of ministry.*

  This means that the people of God experience the power, variety and diversity of 'the pure Word of God'. Without it, the church might promote dead orthodoxy, by muzzling the transformative power of the Spirit-inspired Scriptures.

- *It provides responses to God that express Bible truths and use Bible words.*

  This aids in the long-term learning of Biblical Christianity and the internalisation and reception of Biblical truth. Without it, there is a danger of a church focused on information and opinions, without inner transformation.

These Biblical dynamics are mutually supportive, and mutually enriching, and together they enable 'the very pure Word of God' to form God's people.

3.1 Reformed Anglican theory and practice

This intentional and structured use of the Bible was characteristically Anglican, and marked the distinction between the Reformed and Puritan Anglican tradition and non-Anglican Puritans. Other Puritans required that churches only engage in practices commanded in the Bible, and objected to non-Biblical practices within the Church of England.[1] As we have seen, the Anglican Reformed use of the Bible was significantly different. It held that to be Biblical meant to conform to Biblical doctrine, and included in that category consequences and expressions of Biblical truth. It opposed and precluded un-Biblical and anti-Biblical ideas and practices. It was not restricted to only obeying express instructions of Scripture, but could do and say things not prescribed in Scripture, as long as they expressed Bible truth, and did not contradict it, and as long as everything was done for edification. It held to the God-given means of grace, the scriptures, the ministry, and the sacraments. However it held that the sacraments were to be done in strict obedience to Biblical instructions. The God-given means should be received in God-given ways. It also held that the Bible should be regularly read and preached, that the Bible should be used in our response to God in services, and that extra-Biblical sources could also be used if they expressed Biblical doctrines.[2]

Some may not expect to find this comprehensive commitment to Biblical practice in 1662, because they remember that so many good clergy left the Church of England rather than use the Book. About 1,760 parish clergy and 200 lecturers, schoolteachers and university clergy did leave between 1660 and 1662.[3] However just

---

[1]   And the Congregationalists insisted on congregational autonomy, the Baptists insisted on baptism only of believers, and the Presbyterians insisted on Presbyterian church order.

[2]   For background on Anglicans and the Bible, see Rowan A. Greer, *Anglican Approaches to Scripture: from the reformation to the present*, (New York: Crossroad, 2006); and for insights into the 1662 view, see Trevor Lloyd, 'Worship and the Bible', in Colin Buchanan, Trevor Lloyd and Harold Miller, eds., *Anglican Worship Today*, (London: Collins, 1980), pp. 14-19.

[3]   John Spurr, *The Restoration Church of England, 1646-1689*, (New Haven and London: Yale University Press, 1991), p. 43. The 1,760 parish clergy who left represented about 20% of the parish clergy of the Church of England. See Bray, *Documents*, p. 547.

as many stayed,[4] and these clergy still represented a significant force in the Church of England. The decision whether to leave was a complex one, and their departures had a variety of meanings. While we should honour those who left for the sake of gospel conscience, we should also honour those who stayed for equally good reasons.[5]

I am not claiming that the BCP was a perfect expression of Biblical and Reformed faith and practice. Reformed and Puritan Anglicans have never been satisfied that the reformation of the church has been completed. In William Fuller's 'Booke to the queene', he complains that Queen Elizabeth 'hath so insufficientlie heard, believed, and taken to heart what God hath commanded you, and so weakly and coldly obeyed', that 'but halflie by your majesty hath God been honoured, his church reformed and established, his people taught and comforted.'[6] There has often been unease about some features of successive forms of the Prayer Book, including the retention of the word 'Priest', its optimistic attitude and language in the Baptism and Funeral services, and even the retention of Bishops.

In regard to the retention of the word 'priest', I think that we need to keep in mind the important function of Old Testament priests as teachers of the Law of Moses,[7] and the fact that the ministry of 'priests' as outlined in BCP is so clearly non-sacerdotal, as is the theology of Holy Communion. Bishop Ryle has left us some wise insights on issues to do with the services of Baptism and Funerals,[8] as has Paul Avis on the theology of Bishops[9].

---

[4]   John Spurr, *English Puritanism, 1603-1689*, (Houndmills: Macmillan, 1998), p. 131.
[5]   See my forthcoming St Antholin's Lecture for 2012, *Gospel trials in 1662: to stay or to go*.
[6]   William Fuller, 'Booke to the queen, The Second part of a Register', ii. 52, quoted in Collinson, *Elizabethan Puritan Movement*, p. 29.
[7]   Deuteronomy 33:9,10, Ezra 7, Nehemiah 8, Haggai 2:10-13, Malachi 2: 1-9.
[8]   J.C. Ryle, *Knots Untied: being plan statements on disputed points in religion from the standpoint of an Evangelical Churchman*, (Cambridge: James Clarke, 1977), chapters. V-VII, and Ryle, *Principles for Churchmen*, (London: C.J. Thynne, 1900), chapters VIII-IX.
[9]   Paul Avis, *Anglicanism and the Christian Church*, (Edinburgh: T&T Clark, 1989), pp. 306-311.

3.2 *Why is this comprehensive Biblical character so important?*

It is because Christ is known, and God is known, when the Bible is known. If the Bible is not known, Christ is not known, and if Christ is not known, then God is not known. The 20th Century theologian James Smart wrote that, 'without the Bible the remembered Christ becomes the imagined Christ, (a Christ shaped) by the religiosity and unconscious desires of his worshippers'.[10] And, as we have already seen, John Donne warned that to lose preaching is to risk losing Christ:

> (S)o how long soever Christ have dwelt in any State, or any Church, if he grows speechless, he is departing: if there be a discontinuing, or slackening of preaching, there is a danger of losing Christ.[11]

Hilary of Poitiers clarified our dependence on God's self-revelation in Scripture in these words:

> Since then we are to discourse of the things of God, let us assume that God has full knowledge of Himself, and bow with humble reverence to His words. For He Whom we can only know through His own utterances is the fitting witness concerning Himself.[12]

We are constantly warned in the New Testament how easy it is to lose the gospel, to stray from the truth, to turn aside to error and delusion. For as Bishop J.C. Ryle wrote:

> The Gospel in fact is a most curiously and delicately compounded medicine, and is a medicine that is very easily spoiled.

> You may spoil the Gospel by substitution. You have only to with draw from the eyes of the sinner the grand object which the Bible proposes to Faith, – Jesus Christ; and to substitute another object in His place, – the Church, the Ministry......and

---

[10] James D. Smart, *The Strange Silence of the Bible in the Church*, (London: SCM, 1970), p. 25.
[11] Donne, *Sermons*, VII, p. 157.
[12] Hilary, *De Trinitate*, 1.18. http://www.newadvent.org/fathers/3302.htm

the mischief is done.

You may spoil the Gospel by addition. You only have to add to Christ, the grand object of faith, some other objects as equally worthy of honour, and the mischief is done.....

You may spoil the Gospel by disproportion. You only have to attach an exaggerated importance to the secondary things of Christianity, and a diminished importance to the first things, and the mischief is done. Once alter the proportion of the parts of the truth, and truth soon becomes downright error....

Lastly, but not least, you may completely spoil the Gospel by confused and contradictory directions. Complicated and obscure statements about faith, baptism, and the benefits of the Lord's Supper, all jumbled together, and thrown down without order before hearers, make the Gospel no Gospel at all.[13]

We may also spoil the Gospel by *subtraction*, not least in its polite version, in which Gospel ingredients are not contradicted, but just neglected, ignored and not mentioned! This is 'heresy by silence'.

3.3   Concluding appeals

The 1662 BCP sets a standard for us, which many informal services fail to attain. There is no room for services which are little more than a warm-up for a sermon; no room for services which are full of praise and worship but leave no time for the reading and preaching of the Scriptures; no room for services which reflect the belief that it is the experience of worship (whether Catholic or charismatic) that enables us to enter the presence of God, when our access to God comes through Christ our great high priest, and a believing response to the word of God; no room for services which do not include wide-ranging intercessions for the church and world; no room for services which

---

[13]   Summarised from Ryle, 'Evangelical Religion', in *Knots Untied*, pp. 12-13.

focus entirely on relating to each other; and no room for services which leave no room for praising God[14].

Let me address some words to those who are less sympathetic to this Biblical and Reformed interpretation of Anglicanism and of *The Book of Common Prayer*.

The model of church life and ministry found in the 1662 BCP expresses the theology and practice outlined in the Pastoral Epistles, 1 and 2 Timothy and Titus. This is significant, because those epistles provide most of the New Testament evidence on what ministry looks like after the apostles. The Reformed tradition of Anglicanism expresses this more successfully than do other traditions within Anglicanism, such as the Anglo-Catholic, the Liberal Catholic, the Charismatic, or non-doctrinal Anglicanism.[15] *The Book of Common Prayer* is a significant aspect of our past, and a significant aspect of our identity as Anglicans. We should learn from it, and the recovery of its four Biblical dynamics would lead to a healthy renewal within our church.

Now some words to those who value the Biblical and Reformed tradition of Anglicanism, but who do not use the BCP, and who have moved to more informal services and extempore prayers.

While Western society prides itself in encouraging each individual to find and express who they are, in fact we produce conformist sub-cultures. Similarly, while spontaneity and extempore prayers are meant to enable variety, in fact they tend to lead to predictability and conformity! And we might well wonder if the style of language used for private prayers of small groups of friends will bear the weight of large gatherings of people of different ages.

---

[14] See, Mark Ashton and C.J. Davis, 'Following in Cranmer's Footsteps', in Carson, *Worship by the Book*, pp. 64-168. David Peterson, *Engaging with God: A biblical theology of worship*, (Leicester: Apollos, 1992), gives a helpful insights into Biblical principles and priorities. And, from a different perspective, see Mark Dalby, 'The Reformation Prayer Book Ideal', in Michael Perham, *The Renewal of Common Prayer: Unity and Diversity in the Church of England Worship*, (London: SPCK and Church House Publishing, 1993), pp. 18-26.

[15] I am grateful to the Revd. R.C. Lucas for this observation. See further, Peter Adam, 'The Scriptures are God's Voice: the Church is His Echo', in B.N. Kaye [ed.], *Wonderfully and Confessedly Strange: Australian Essays in Anglican Ecclesiology*, (Hindmarsh: ATF Press, 2006), pp. 81-102.

A significant problem for some contemporary services is that those who lead them are untrained and unprepared for their ministries. This is not their fault. We need ministers to commit to upgrading the quality of their services by preparing and training all who will lead, and by good preparation for each service. A high level of lay involvement needs to be matched by the necessary gifts, and by training for ministry. When we do have a 'precomposed' prayer, we must train service leaders to say, 'We now pray this prayer (or these words)', not, 'We now read this prayer'!

And I hope that those who have discarded 1662 will think again. There are some contexts of ministry, such as with elderly people, where using this Book still makes perfect sense. And younger people have an enviable ability to enjoy both the antique and the contemporary, and may well be attracted to the venerable antiquity of BCP. They might enjoy BCP, with Reggae or Heavy Metal, combined with a 40 minute expository sermon, meeting in a café with stainglass windows! They have the ability to enjoy mixtures that their elders find bewildering!

Many people today of all ages find contemporary spontaneous un-prepared services lacking in Biblical depth and maturity, and are recovering or discovering the joys of the Biblical substance of the 1662 Book. Any replacement must match its standards.

Good services take time and energy, and the determination to bring honour to God and edification to his people, and to preach Christ in all that happens. *The Book of Common Prayer* sets a standard for us, that of 'the very pure Word of God': we would do well to work to the same standard and purpose, with God's help, and for God's glory.

Bibliography

- *Certain Homilies or Sermons appointed to be read in Churches in the time of Queen Elizabeth*, (London: SPCK, 1864).
- The Book of Common Prayer, together with the Ordering of Bishops, Priests and Deacons, and the Articles of Religion. http://www.churchofengland.org/prayer-worship/worship/book-of-common-prayer.aspx 7th May 2012.
- The Canons of the Church of England. http://www.churchofengland.org/about-us/structure/churchlawlegis/canons/canons-7th-edition.aspx 7th May 2012
- The Decrees of the Council of Trent http://history.hanover.edu/texts/trent.html 7th May 2012.

Adam, Peter, 'A Church "Halfly Reformed": the Puritan Dilemma', republished in Lee Gatiss, (ed.), *Pilgrims, Warriors, and Servants: Puritan Wisdom for Today's Church, The St Antholin's Lectures, Volume 1 1991-2000*, (London: The Latimer Trust, 2010), pp. 185-216.

Adam, Peter, 'To bring men to heaven by preaching: John Donne's Evangelistic Sermons', republished in Lee Gatiss, (ed.), *Preachers, Pastors, and Ambassadors: Puritan Wisdom for Today's Church, The St Antholin's Lectures, Volume II, 2001-2010*, (London: The Latimer Trust, 2011), pp. 261-292.

Adam, Peter, 'Word and Spirit: the Puritan-Quaker Debate', in Lee Gatiss, (ed.), *Preachers, Pastors, and Ambassadors: Puritan Wisdom for Today's Church, The St Antholin's Lectures, Volume II, 2001-2010*, (London: The Latimer Trust, 2011), pp. 49-96.

Adam, Peter, 'The Scriptures are God's Voice: the Church is His Echo', in B.N. Kaye, (ed.), *Wonderfully and Confessedly Strange: Australian Essays in Anglican Ecclesiology*, (Hindmarsh: ATF Press, 2006), pp. 81-102.

Adams, Thomas, *An Exposition of 2 Peter*, (Birmingham: Solid Ground Christian Books, 2008).

Ashton, Mark and Davis, C.J., 'Following in Cranmer's Footsteps', in D.A. Carson, (ed.), *Worship by the Book*, (Grand Rapids: Zondervan, 2002), pp. 64-168.

Atherstone, Andrew, *Charles Simeon on "The Excellency of the Liturgy"*, (Norwich: Canterbury Press, 2012).

Atkinson, Nigel, *Richard Hooker and the Authority of Scripture, Tradition and Reason*, (Carlisle: Paternoster, 1997).

Avis, Paul, *Anglicanism and the Christian Church*, (Edinburgh: T&T Clark, 1989).

Augustine of Hippo, *Contra Faustum*, Book XVII, 3, http://www.newadvent.org/fathers/140617.htm, 7th May 2012

Benn, Wallace, 'Ussher on Bishops: A Reforming ecclesiology', in Lee Gatiss, (ed.), *Preachers, Pastors, and Ambassadors: Puritan Wisdom for Today's Church, St Antholin's Lectures, Volume 2, 2001-2010* (London: The Latimer Trust, 2011), pp. 97-122.

Bray, Gerald, *The Faith We Confess: An Exposition of the Thirty-Nine Articles*, (London: The Latimer Trust, 2009).

Bray, Gerald, (ed.), *Documents of the English Reformation*, (Minneapolis: Fortress Press, 1994).

Calder, Isabel M., *Activities of the Puritan Faction of the Church of England 1625-33*, (London: SPCK, 1957).

Calvin, John, *Institutes of the Christian Religion*, vol. 1, tr. Ford Lewis Battles, The Library of Christian Classics, Vol. XX, (Philadelphia: Westminster Press, 1960).

Calvin, John, *Preface to the Psalms*, in *Commentaries on The Book of Joshua and the Psalms of David and others*, Calvin Translation Society, Vol. IV, (Reprinted, Grand Rapids: Baker, 1981).

Calvin, John, *Commentary on the Four Books of Moses*, Calvin Translation Society, Vol. III. (Reprinted, Grand Rapids: Baker, 1981).

Carroll, Thomas K., *Preaching the Word: The Message of the Fathers of the Church*, (Wilmington: Michael Glazier, 1984).

Carson, D.A., (ed.), *Worship by the Book*, (Grand Rapids: Zondervan, 2002).

Cinnamond, Andrew, *What Matters in Reforming the Church? Puritan Grievances under Elizabeth I*, St Antholin Lectureship, (London: the Latimer Trust, 2011).

Collinson, Patrick, *The Elizabethan Puritan Movement*, (London: Jonathan Cape, 1967).

Collinson, Patrick, *Archbishop Grindal 1519-1583: The Struggle for a Reformed Church*, (London: Jonathan Cape, 1979).

Cranmer, Thomas, *Writing and Disputations of Thomas Cranmer...Relative to the Sacrament of the Lord's Supper*, The Parker Society, (ed.), J.E. Cox, (Cambridge: The University Press, 1844).

Cranmer, Thomas, *Miscellaneous Writings and Letters of Thomas Cranmer*, The Parker Society, (ed.), J.E. Cox, (Cambridge: The University Press, 1846).

Dalby, Mark, 'The Reformation Prayer Book Ideal', in Michael Perham, (ed.), *The Renewal of Common Prayer: Unity and Diversity in the Church of England Worship*, (London: SPCK and Church House Publishing, 1993), pp. 18-26.

Davies, Horton, *Worship and Theology in England*, Volume 1, (Grand Rapids: Eerdmans, 1966).

Davies, Julian, *The Caroline captivity of the church: Charles I and the remoulding of Anglicanism 1625-1641*, (Oxford: Clarendon Press, 1992).

Dever, Mark, *Richard Sibbes: Puritanism and Calvinism in Late Elizabethan and Early Stuart England*, (Macon: Mercer University Press, 2000).

Dickens, A.G., *The English Reformation*, (London: Collins, 1967).

Dix, Gregory, *The Shape of the Liturgy*, (London: Dacre Press, 1945).

Doerksen, David W., *Conforming to the Word: Herbert, Donne, and the English Church before Laud*, (Lewisburg: Bucknell University Press/London: Associated University Presses, 1997).

Donne, John, *The Sermons of John Donne*, Volumes 1 – 10, eds., M.R. Potter, and E.M. Simpson, (Berkeley: University of California Press, 1953-1962).

Edwards, David L., *John Donne, Man of Flesh and Spirit*, (London and New York: Continuum, 2001).

Fincham, Kenneth, *Prelate as Pastor: the Episcopate of James I*, (Oxford: Oxford University Press, 1990).

Fincham, Kenneth, *The Early Stuart Church 1603-1642*, (Stanford: Stanford University Press, 1993).

Ford, Alan, *James Ussher: theology, history and politics in early-modern Ireland and England*, (Oxford: Oxford University Press, 2007).

Gatiss, Lee, *The True Profession of the Gospel: Augustus Toplady and reclaiming our Reformed foundations*, (London: The Latimer Trust, 2010).

Gatiss, Lee, 'The Grand Nursery of Puritanism: St. Antholin's as a Strategic Centre for Gospel Ministry', in Lee Gatiss, (ed.), *Preachers, Pastors and Ambassadors: Puritan Wisdom for Today's Church, The St Antholin's Lectures, Volume II, 2001-2010*, (London: The Latimer Trust, 2011), pp. 3-48.

Goudge, William, *Commentary on Hebrews*, (Grand Rapids: Kregel, 1980).

Green, V.H.H., *Religion at Oxford and Cambridge*, (London: SCM, 1964).

Greer, Rowan A., *Anglican Approaches to Scripture: from the reformation to the present*, (New York: Crossroad, 2006).

Gribben, Crawford, *The Irish Puritans: James Ussher and the Reformation of the Church*, (Darlington: Evangelical Press, 2003).

Hampton, Stephen, *Anti-Arminians: The Anglican Reformed Tradition from Charles II to George I*, (Oxford: Oxford University Press, 2008).

Hart, D.G. and Mueller, John R., (eds.), *With Reverence and Awe: Returning to the Basics of Reformed Worship*, (Philippsburg: P&R, 2002).

Hutchinson, F.E., (ed.), *The Works of George Herbert*, (Oxford: Clarendon Press, 1941).

Hill, Christopher, *Society and Puritanism in Pre-Revolutionary England*, (London: Panther, 1969).

Hilary of Poitiers, *De Trinitate*, http://www.newadvent.org/fathers/3302.htm 7th May 2012.

Hopkins, Hugh Evan, *Charles Simeon of Cambridge*, (London: Hodder and Stoughton, 1977).

Hughes, Philip Edgcumbe, 'Preaching, Homilies, and Prophesyings in Sixteenth Century England', *Churchman*, 89/1, 1975, pp. 7-32.

Hughes, Philip Edgcumbe, *Theology of the English Reformers*, (London: Hodder and Stoughton, 1965).

Huntley, Frank Livingstone, *Bishop Joseph Hall 1574-1656*, (Cambridge: DS Brewer, 1979).

Hylson-Smith, Kenneth, *Evangelicals in the Church of England, 1734-1984*, (Edinburgh: T&T Clark, 1989).

Jewel, John, *The Works of Bishop Jewel*, (ed.), John Ayer, Vol. IV, (Cambridge: The University Press, 1850).

Jewel, John, *Writings of John Jewel*, (London: Religious Tract Society, nd).

Knox, D.B., *The Thirty-Nine Articles: The historic basis of Anglican Faith*, (London: Hodder and Stoughton, 1967).

Lake, Peter, *Moderate Puritans and the Elizabethan Church*, (Cambridge: Cambridge University Press, 1982).

Leaver, R.A., *The Works of John Marbeck*, (Oxford: Sutton Courtenay Press, 1978).

Leighton, Robert, 'A Practical Commentary on the First Epistle General of St Peter', The Whole Works of Robert Leighton, Vols I, (ed.), J.N. Pearson, (London: James Duncan, 1835).

Lloyd, Trevor, 'Worship and the Bible', in Colin Buchanan, Trevor Lloyd and Harold Miller, (eds.), Anglican Worship Today, (London: Collins, 1980), pp. 14-19.

Luther, Martin, Martin Luther: Selections from his writings, (ed.), John Dillenberger, (New York: Anchor Books, 1961).

MacCulloch, Dairmaid, Building a Godly Realm: The Establishment of English Protestantism, (London: The Historical Association, 1992).

MacCulloch, Dairmaid, The Boy King: Edward VI and the Protestant Reformation, (New York: Palgrave, 1999).

MacCulloch, Dairmaid, Thomas Cranmer: A Life, (New Haven and London: Yale University Press, 1996).

Mantel, Hilary, Wolf Hall, (London: Fourth Estate, 2009).

Manwaring, Randle, From Controversy to Co-existence: Evangelicals in the Church of England 1914-1980, (Cambridge: Cambridge University Press, 1985).

Mueller, William R., John Donne: Preacher, (Princeton: Princeton University Press, 1962).

Myers, Jacob M., Ezra, Nehemiah, The Anchor Bible, (New York: Doubleday, 1965).

Null, Ashley, The Thirty-Nine Articles and Reformation Anglicanism, (Mukono: Uganda Christian University, 2005).

Null, Ashley, 'Thomas Cranmer and Tudor Evangelicalism', in Michael A.G. Haykin and Kenneth J. Stewart, (eds.), The Emergence of Evangelicalism: Exploring Historical Continuities, (Nottingham: Apollos, 2008), pp. 221-251.

O'Donovan, Oliver, On the Thirty-Nine Articles: A Conversation with Tudor Christianity, (Exeter: Paternoster Press, 1993).

Packer, James I. and Beckwith, Roger T., The Thirty-Nine Articles: their Place and Use Today, 2nd edition (London: Latimer Trust, 2006).

Papazian, Mary Arshagouni, John Donne and the Protestant Reformation: New Perspectives, (Detroit: Wayne State University Press, 2003).

Parker, T.H.L., Calvin's Preaching, (Edinburgh: T&T Clark, 1992).

Parsons, Martin, The Holy Communion: An Exposition of the Prayer Book Service, The Prayer Book Commentaries, (London: Hodder and Stoughton, 1961).

Parsons, Martin, The Ordinal: An Exposition of the Ordination Services, The Prayer Book Commentaries, (London: Hodder and Stoughton, 1964).

Peterson, David, Engaging with God: A biblical theology of worship, (Leicester: Apollos, 1992).

Pilkington, James, 'Exposition upon the Prophet Haggai, Exposition upon the Prophet Obadiah, Exposition upon certain chapter in Nehemiah', in The Works of James Pilkington, The Parker Society, (Cambridge: The University Press, 1842), pp. 1-496.

Primus, John H., Richard Greenham: the portrait of an Elizabethan pastor, (Macon: Mercer University Press, 1998).

Ramsey, A.M., The Gospel and the Catholic Church, (London: Longmans, Green, 1956).

Ramsey, A.M., *From Gore to Temple: The Development of Anglican Theology between Lux Mundi and the Second World War 1889-1939*, (London: Longmans, 1960).

Ryle, J.C., *Knots Untied: being plan statements on disputed points in religion from the standpoint of an Evangelical Churchman,* (Cambridge: James Clarke, 1977).

Ryle, J.C., *Principles for Churchmen,* (London: C.J. Thynne, 1900).

Samuel, David, (ed.), *The Evangelical Succession in the Church of England,* (Cambridge: James Clarke, 1979).

Seaver, Paul S., *The Puritan Lectureships,* (Stanford: Stanford University Press, 1970).

Smart, James D., *The Strange Silence of the Bible in the Church,* (London: SCM, 1970).

Spurr, John *The Restoration Church of England, 1646-1689,* (New Haven and London: Yale University Press, 1991).

Spurr, John, *English Puritanism, 1603-1689,* (Houndmills: Macmillan, 1998).

Stephens-Hodge, L.E.H., *The Collects: An Introduction and Exposition, The Prayer Book Commentaries,* (London: Hodder and Stoughton, 1966).

Stibbs, A.M., *Sacrament, Sacrifice and Eucharist: the Meaning Function and Use of the Lord's Supper,* (London: The Tyndale Press, 1961).

Stott, John R.W., *Canticles and Selected Psalms, The Prayer Book Commentaries,* (London: Hodder and Stoughton, 1966).

Sykes, Stephen, 'The Anglican Character' in Ian Bunting, (ed.), *Celebrating the Anglican Way,* (London: Hodder and Stoughton, 1996), pp. 21-32.

Thomas, Griffith W.H., *The Principles of Theology: An Introduction to the Thirty-Nine Articles*, (Oregon: Wipf and Stock Publishers, 2005).

Turnbull, Richard, *Anglican and Evangelical?* (London: Continuum, 2007).

Tyacke, Nicholas, *Aspects of English Protestantism, c.1530-1700,* (Manchester: Manchester University Press, 2001).

Webster, Tom, *Godly Clergy in Early Stuart England: The Caroline Puritan Movement c1620-1643,* (Cambridge: Cambridge University Press, 1997).

Wesley, John, *John Wesley's Prayer Book,* www.vulcanhammer.org/whats-important-in-christianity/1662-book-of-common-prayer/ 7th May 2012

White, James F. [ed], *The Sunday Service Book of the Methodists in North America* (Cleveland: OSL Publications, 1991).

Williams, John, *The Work of Archbishop John Williams,* (ed.), Barrie Williams, (Abingdon: Sutton Courtenay Press, 1980).

Zahl, Paul F.M., *The Protestant Face of Anglicanism,* (Grand Rapids/Cambridge: Eerdmans, 1998).

Latimer Publications

Latimer Studies

LATIMER PUBLICATIONS

Latimer Publications

Latimer Briefings

LB01	The Church of England: What it is, and what it stands for	R. T. Beckwith
LB02	Praying with Understanding: Explanations of Words and Passages in the Book of Common Prayer	R. T. Beckwith
LB03	The Failure of the Church of England? The Church, the Nation and the Anglican Communion	A. Pollard
LB04	Towards a Heritage Renewed	H.R.M. Craig
LB05	Christ's Gospel to the Nations: The Heart & Mind of Evangelicalism Past, Present & Future	Peter Jensen
LB06	Passion for the Gospel: Hugh Latimer (1485–1555) Then and Now. A commemorative lecture to mark the 450th anniversary of his martyrdom in Oxford	A. McGrath
LB07	Truth and Unity in Christian Fellowship	Michael Nazir-Ali
LB08	Unworthy Ministers: Donatism and Discipline Today	Mark Burkill
LB09	Witnessing to Western Muslims: A Worldview Approach to Sharing Faith	Richard Shumack
LB10	Scarf or Stole at Ordination? A Plea for the Evangelical Conscience	Andrew Atherstone

Latimer Books

GGC	God, Gays and the Church: Human Sexuality and Experience in Christian Thinking	eds. Lisa Nolland, Chris Sugden, Sarah Finch
WTL	The Way, the Truth and the Life: Theological Resources for a Pilgrimage to a Global Anglican Future	eds. Vinay Samuel, Chris Sugden, Sarah Finch
AEID	Anglican Evangelical Identity – Yesterday and Today	J.I.Packer and N.T.Wright
IB	The Anglican Evangelical Doctrine of Infant Baptism	John Stott and J.Alec Motyer
BF	Being Faithful: The Shape of Historic Anglicanism Today	Theological Resource Group of GAFCON
TPG	The True Profession of the Gospel: Augustus Toplady and Reclaiming our Reformed Foundations	Lee Gatiss
SG	Shadow Gospel: Rowan Williams and the Anglican Communion Crisis	Charles Raven
TTB	Translating the Bible: From Willliam Tyndale to King James	Gerald Bray
PWS	Pilgrims, Warriors, and Servants: Puritan Wisdom for Today's Church	ed. Lee Gatiss
PPA	Preachers, Pastors, and Ambassadors: Puritan Wisdom for Today's Church	ed. Lee Gatiss
CWP	The Church, Women Bishops and Provision: The Integrity of Orthodox Objections to the Proposed Legislation Allowing Women Bishops	

Anglican Foundations Series

FWC	The Faith We Confess: An Exposition of the 39 Articles	Gerald Bray
AF02	The 'Very Pure Word of God': The Book of Common Prayer as a Model of Biblical Liturgy	Peter Adam
AF03	Dearly Beloved: Building God's People Through Morning and Evening Prayer	Mark Burkill
AF04	Day By Day: The Rhythm of the Bible in the Book of Common Prayer	Benjamin Sargent

Lightning Source UK Ltd.
Milton Keynes UK
UKOW051436020712

195356UK00001B/7/P